Wuthering Heights

EMILY BRONTË

Level 5

Retold by Evelyn Attwood
Series Editors: Andy Hopkins and Jocelyn Potter

Pearson Education Limited
Edinburgh Gate, Harlow,
Essex CM20 2JE, England
and Associated Companies throughout the world.

ISBN 0 582 419441

First published in the Longman Simplified English Series 1978
First published in Longman Fiction 1993
This adaptation first published 1996
Second impression 1997
This edition first published 1999

7 9 10 8 6

NEW EDITION

Set in 11/14pt Bembo
Printed in China
SWTC/06

Published by Pearson Education Limited in association with
Penguin Books Ltd, both companies being subsidiaries of Pearson Plc

For a complete list of titles available in the Penguin Readers series, please write to your local
Pearson Education office or to: Penguin Readers Marketing Department,
Pearson Education, Edinburgh Gate, Harlow, Essex CM20 2JE.

Contents

Introduction

Emily Jane Brontë was born in Yorkshire, England, in 1818, the fifth of six children in a family of writers. Their father, Patrick, was an Irishman who became the minister of a church in Haworth in 1820. Their mother, Maria Branwell, died in 1821, and her older sister came to look after the household. Mr Brontë himself educated Branwell, the one boy in the family, at home. But their aunt was not able to deal with the girls' education and in 1824 Maria and Elizabeth were sent away to a religious school in Cowan Bridge, where Charlotte and Emily joined them later. Conditions at the school were difficult and Maria and Elizabeth were taken ill and sent home. Maria died in May 1825 and Elizabeth in June of the same year. Charlotte and Emily were then taken away from the school.

For the next five years the four remaining children stayed at home. Branwell received lessons from his father and the girls, Charlotte, Emily and Anne, educated themselves as well as they could. The children all read widely. They saw little of other families and to make their dull life in the small village where they lived more interesting, they began to invent stories. Many of those stories still exist today.

In 1831 Charlotte went away to school again, returning a year later to teach her sisters. She went back to the school as a teacher in 1835 and took Emily with her, but she found teaching difficult both at the school and in the two positions as governess that followed. During this period she had two offers of marriage, which she refused. She was keen to open a school of her own, and in 1842 she went to Belgium with Emily to improve her French. When their aunt died, the girls returned home. Charlotte then went back to Brussels by herself but was lonely, became ill and left again for Haworth. Her brother Branwell had failed at every job he tried and increasingly turned to alcohol and drugs. To add to her unhappiness, Charlotte's attempts to open a school in Haworth failed.

In 1846, Charlotte persuaded her sisters Emily and Anne to allow their poems to appear in a book with her own poems. The book, which they paid for themselves, was not a financial success, but they all continued to write. Charlotte's story *Jane Eyre* came out first, in 1847, and was an immediate popular success. Later the same year Anne's *Agnes Grey* and Emily's *Wuthering Heights* appeared.

Branwell died in September 1848. At his funeral Emily caught a fever and became very ill. She died in December. Anne died in May of the following year, at Scarborough, where she had hoped the sea air would help to improve her health. In spite of these terrible events, Charlotte struggled on with her writing and managed to complete two more books. She married in 1854, but died a year later. Her husband continued to look after Mr Brontë, who lived longer than all his children and died at the age of eighty-four.

Wuthering Heights is Emily Brontë's only full-length story. It is set on the wild and lonely Yorkshire moors that Emily knew and loved more than any of her sisters. The book is an imaginative and moving story, but was not well received when it first appeared. It was criticized as being cruel and miserable. The rough, hard emotions that fire the book are completely different from the gentle touch and polite subject matter of most stories written at the time. It was considered especially shocking that such scenes had been written by a woman. Only later was the book recognized as one of the most powerful and important works of fiction of the nineteenth century.

Wuthering Heights is the name of an old house, set high up on the wind-swept Yorkshire moors. At the end of the eighteenth century it is home to the Earnshaw family. Another family, the Lintons, live in the valley at the more comfortable Thrushcross Grange. Mr Earnshaw, father of Catherine and Hindley, goes to Liverpool one day on business and brings home with him a child who has been living on the streets in the worst part of the city. Mr Earnshaw takes the child as his son, giving him the name of Heathcliff. Nothing is the same again. A chain of events begins which splits both families apart. Heathcliff's influence on the family, and particularly his emotional relationship with Catherine, the strong-willed daughter of the household, drive this beautiful and powerful story.

PART 1   A STRANGE HOUSEHOLD (NOVEMBER 1801)

Told by Mr Lockwood, tenant of Thrushcross Grange

Chapter 1   A Rough Welcome

I have just returned from a visit to my landlord, the only neighbour I shall have for many miles. In all England, I don't believe I could have fixed on a country house more distant from society.

Mr Heathcliff and I are a suitable pair to share this loneliness. As I rode up, his black eyes stared at me in a most unfriendly manner from under his dark forehead.

'Mr Heathcliff?' I said.

He nodded.

'I am Mr Lockwood, your new tenant at Thrushcross Grange, sir. I felt I should call on you as soon as possible after my arrival.'

He made no offer to shake hands. His hands remained in his pocket.

'Walk in!' He spoke with closed teeth, and continued to lean over the gate. When he saw my horse's chest pushing against it, he did take out his hand to unchain it, and then walked in front of me up the stone path, calling, as we entered the yard: 'Joseph, take Mr Lockwood's horse, and bring up some wine.'

'There must be only one servant,' I thought. 'That must be why the grass is growing up between the stones, and the plants are growing wild.'

Joseph seemed an unpleasant old man. 'The Lord help us!' he murmured in a disapproving voice, as he took my horse.

Wuthering Heights is the name of Mr Heathcliff's house. 'Wuthering' is a local word, used to describe the wildness of the weather in this part of Yorkshire in time of storm. One may guess the power of the north wind by the way the few poorly grown trees at the end of the house lean towards the ground, and by a row of bushes all stretching their branches in one direction, as if begging for the warmth of the sun.

Before I entered the house, I paused to admire some unusual decorative stonework over the front. Above it I saw the date '1500' and the name 'Hareton Earnshaw'. I would have asked for a few details about the place, but the owner appeared impatient.

One step brought us into the family sitting room. On the wall at one end there was row after row of large metal dishes, with silver pots and drinking cups right up to the roof. There was no ceiling. Above the fireplace were several evil-looking guns. The floor was of smooth white stone. The chairs were high-backed and painted green. In a corner lay a large dog and her young ones. Other, smaller dogs sat in other corners.

The room and furniture would have been nothing out of the ordinary if they had belonged to a simple Yorkshire farmer, but Mr Heathcliff seems out of place in his home and way of living. He is a dark-skinned gypsy in appearance, but in manners and dress a gentleman: that is, as much a gentleman as many country landowners – rather careless of his dress, perhaps, but upright and good-looking. His expression is rather severe and unsmiling.

I took a seat by the fire and filled up a few minutes of silence by trying to make friends with the largest dog.

'You'd better leave her alone,' said Heathcliff roughly, pushing the animal away with his foot, as she showed me all her teeth. Then, crossing to a side door, he shouted again, 'Joseph!'

Joseph murmured in the room below, but gave no sign of returning, so his master went down after him, leaving me face to face with the dogs, who watched all my movements. I sat still, but could not help showing my dislike of the animals, and soon the biggest jumped at my knees. I knocked her back, and got the table between us. This excited the others, who ran to join in. I was surrounded, and had to call for help.

Mr Heathcliff and his man were slow to answer. Luckily, a big strong woman with red cheeks rushed in from the kitchen and drove off the attack with a cooking pan. Heathcliff entered shortly after that.

'What the devil is the matter?' he asked.

I gave him my opinion of his dogs.

'They won't attack people who touch nothing,' he remarked, putting a bottle in front of me, and moving the table back into position. 'The dogs are right to be watchful. Take a glass of wine.'

'No, thank you.'

'Not bitten, are you?'

'If I had been, I would have left my mark on the biter!'

Heathcliff laughed.

'Come, come,' he said, 'you are upset, Mr Lockwood. Here, take a little wine. Guests are so rare in this house that I and my dogs, I'm prepared to admit, hardly know how to receive them. Your health, sir!'

I smiled, beginning to see that it was foolish to be annoyed by a lot of badly behaved dogs, and unprepared to provide my host with further amusement by losing my temper.

He probably realized the foolishness of offending a good tenant. He began to talk with greater politeness, and on a subject that he supposed might interest me. I found him very intelligent, and before I went home I was ready to offer another visit tomorrow. He showed no further wish for my company, but I shall go in spite of this.

Chapter 2   Even Less Welcome

Yesterday afternoon was misty and cold. I nearly decided to spend it by my sitting room fire, but when I came up from dinner the servant was still trying to light it. I took my hat and, after a four-mile walk, arrived at Heathcliff's garden gate just in time to escape the first light feathers of a snowfall.

On that cold hill-top the earth was frozen hard and the air made me shiver. I knocked on the front door, and the dogs began to make a noise.

I knocked a second time. The head of the unfriendly Joseph appeared out of a round window of the storehouse.

'What do you want?' he shouted. 'The master's down at the farm.'

'Is there nobody to open the door?' I called.

'There's only the mistress, and she won't open, even if you shout until night-time.'

'Why? Can't you tell her who I am?'

'It's not my business.' His head disappeared.

The snow began to fall thickly. I was about to knock a third time, when a young man without a coat and carrying a spade came from the yard behind the house.

He called to me to follow him and, after marching through a wash-house and an area containing a coalhouse and a pump, we at last arrived in the large, warm cheerful room in which I was received before.

A fire was burning and near the table, which was laid for an evening meal, I was pleased to see the 'mistress'.

I greeted her and waited, thinking she would ask me to take a seat. She looked at me, leaning back in her chair, and remained silent and still.

'It's rough weather,' I remarked. 'I had hard work, Mrs Heathcliff, to make your servant hear me.'

4

She never opened her mouth, but kept her eyes on me in an extremely unpleasant manner.

'Sit down,' said the young man roughly. 'He'll be in soon.'

I obeyed.

One of the dogs now came up in a more friendly manner than before.

'A beautiful animal,' I began again. 'Do you intend to keep the little ones, Mrs Heathcliff?'

'They are not mine,' said the mistress of the house, more rudely than Heathcliff himself.

I repeated my remark on the wildness of the weather.

'You shouldn't have come out,' said the lady, rising and reaching two painted tea boxes from the shelf above the fireplace.

Her position until she stood up had been sheltered from the light. Now I had a clear view of her whole face and figure. She seemed little more than a girl, with an admirable form and the most delicate little face that I had ever had the pleasure of seeing.

The boxes were almost out of her reach. I made a movement to help her. She turned on me.

'I don't want your help,' she said sharply.

I quickly begged her pardon.

'Were you asked to tea?' she demanded, standing with a spoonful of tea held over the pot.

'No,' I said, half smiling. 'You are the proper person to ask me.'

She threw the tea back, spoon and all, and returned to her chair. Her lower lip was pushed out, like a child's, ready to cry.

The young man was looking down on me fiercely.

I began to doubt that he was a servant. Both his dress and his speech were rough, his hair was uncut, and his hands were as brown as a farm worker's; but his manner was free, almost proud, and he showed no sign of serving the lady of the house.

Five minutes later, Heathcliff arrived.

'I am surprised that you chose the thick of a snowstorm to

walk out in,' he said, shaking the white powder from his clothes. 'Do you know you run the risk of being lost? Even people familiar with these moors often lose their way on an evening like this.'

'Perhaps I can get a guide from among your boys? Could you do without one for a few hours?'

'No, I could not.'

'Are you going to make the tea?' asked the young man, looking at the lady.

'Is *he* to have any?' she asked, turning to Heathcliff.

'Get it ready, will you?' was the answer, so fiercely spoken that I moved in surprise.

When the preparations were completed, he invited me to join them: 'Now, sir, bring your chair forward.'

We all pulled out chairs round the table, and the meal began without further conversation.

I could not believe that they sat together every day in such an unfriendly silence. If I had caused the cloud, I thought, it was my duty to try to drive it away.

'Many could not imagine living in happiness so far from society,' I began, 'but you, Mr Heathcliff, with your wife—'

'My wife is no longer alive, sir.'

I realized that I had made a mistake. I looked at the young man.

'Mrs Heathcliff is my son's wife.' As he spoke, Heathcliff turned a strange look of hate in her direction.

'And this young man . . .'

'Is not my son. My son is dead.'

The youth became red in the face.

'My name is Hareton Earnshaw,' he said roughly, 'and I advise you to respect it!'

He fixed his eye on me in a threatening manner. I began to feel very much out of place in this strange family circle, and I decided to be more careful about risking my presence under its roof a third time.

When the business of eating was over, I went to the window. Dark night was coming on, and the sky and hills were hidden from sight by the wild movement of the snow in the wind.

'I don't think it will be possible for me to get home now without a guide,' I said.

'Hareton, drive those sheep into shelter,' said Heathcliff.

'What must I do?' I continued.

There was no reply and, looking round, I saw only Joseph bringing in the dogs' food and Mrs Heathcliff leaning over the fire.

'Mrs Heathcliff,' I said anxiously, 'you must excuse me for troubling you. Do point out some landmarks by which I may know my way home.'

'Take the road you came by,' she answered, settling herself in a chair with a book and a candle. 'I can't show you the way. They wouldn't let me go beyond the garden wall.'

'Are there no boys at the farm?'

'No. There are only Heathcliff, Earnshaw, Zillah, Joseph and myself.'

'I hope this will be a lesson to you, to make no more foolish journeys on these hills,' cried the voice of Heathcliff from the kitchen. 'As for staying here, I don't keep rooms for visitors.'

'I can sleep on a chair in this room.'

'No! A stranger is a stranger, whether rich or poor. It will not suit me to have anyone wandering round this place when I am not on guard.'

With this insult, my patience was at an end. I pushed past him into the yard. It was so dark that I could not see the way out.

Joseph was milking the cows by the light of a lamp. I seized it and, calling that I would send it back the next day, rushed to the nearest gate.

'Master, master, he's stealing the lamp!' shouted the old man. 'Hold him, dogs, hold him!'

Two hairy animals jumped at my throat, bringing me to the ground and putting out the light, while rude laughter from Heathcliff and Hareton increased the force of my anger and shame. There I was forced to lie until they called the dogs off.

The violence of my anger caused my nose to bleed. Heathcliff continued to laugh, and I continued to shout angrily. At last Zillah, the big woman servant, came out to see what was happening.

'Are we going to murder people right on our doorstep? Look at that poor young gentleman – he can hardly breathe! Come in, and I'll cure that.'

With these words, she suddenly threw some icy water down my neck and pulled me into the kitchen.

I felt sick and faint. Heathcliff told Zillah to give me something strong to drink. I then allowed her to lead me to bed.

Chapter 3   An Uncomfortable Night

On the way upstairs, Zillah advised me to make no noise, as the master had some strange idea about the room she was taking me to, and would never allow anyone to sleep there.

I locked my door and looked around. The only furniture in the room was a chair, a long heavy chest for clothes, and a large wooden box, with square windows cut in the top. I looked inside this piece of furniture, and found it was a strange, ancient kind of bed, forming a little room of its own, the broad edge of which conveniently served as a table. I slid back the doors, got in with my light, and pulled them together again.

The shelf, on which I placed my candle, had a few old books piled up in one corner, and was covered with handwriting. This writing was just a name repeated many times – 'Catherine Earnshaw', sometimes changed to 'Catherine Heathcliff', and then again to 'Catherine Linton'.

I leaned my head against the window and continued to read the names again and again until my eyes closed. I had not rested five minutes, though, before I discovered that my candle had fallen on one of the books, and there was a smell of burning leather. I sat up and examined the book. It had the name 'Catherine Earnshaw' on the first page, and a date about a quarter of a century old. I shut it, and took up another book, and another, until I had examined them all.

The books had been well used, though not always for the usual purpose. Every bit of empty space was filled with childish writing, parts of which took the form of a record of daily happenings. At the top of one page I was highly amused to find an excellent drawing of Joseph. I felt an immediate interest in the unknown Catherine, and I began to read out the faint words:

A terrible Sunday. I wish my father were alive again. Hindley is hateful. His treatment of Heathcliff is terrible.

All day it has been pouring with rain. We could not go to church. While Hindley and his wife sat downstairs by a comfortable fire, we were commanded to take our prayer books and go up to the top of the house to listen to Joseph praying. We stayed there for three hours, but my brother still thought we came down too soon.

'Remember that you have a master here,' he said. 'I'll kill the first person that makes me angry. Oh, boy? Was that you? Frances, pull his hair as you go by.'

Frances did so, then went and sat with her husband. We hid ourselves in a corner but were soon driven out by Joseph, who said we were wicked to start playing on a Sunday. I wrote in this book for twenty minutes, but my companion is impatient and suggests that we should have a run on the moors. We cannot be wetter or colder in the rain than we are here.

I suppose that they did this, as the next sentence began a new subject:

I never thought that Hindley would ever make me cry so! My head aches terribly! Poor Heathcliff! Hindley calls him a gypsy, and won't let him sit with us or eat with us any more. My brother says that Heathcliff and I must not play together, and threatens to turn him out of the house if we disobey his orders. He has been blaming our father for treating Heathcliff too kindly, and swears he will reduce him to his right place.

My head began to fall over the yellowed page. My eye wandered on, but I soon sank back in bed and fell asleep.

Oh, the effects of bad tea and bad temper! What else could have caused me to pass such an uncomfortable night?

One horrible dream followed another . . . Joseph was guiding me home. He led me instead to the church I had passed on my way to the Heights. The priest's talk was divided into 490 parts. I became tired and restless: my head began to drop. In a voice of thunder he called on all his listeners to punish me for my wickedness. All the churchgoers rushed at me with uplifted sticks, and I, having no weapon, began struggling with my nearest attacker, Joseph. The church was full of the sound of blows . . .

The blows sounded so loud that I awoke.

What had caused the noise? A branch of a tree touching my window.

I turned in my bed, and slept again. This time, I remembered where I was lying, and I heard the sound of the wind and the branch on the window. It annoyed me so much that I was determined to silence it. I got up and tried to open the window, but without success.

'I must stop it, in spite of that!' I murmured, breaking the glass with my hand and stretching it out to seize the annoying branch.

Instead, my fingers closed on the fingers of a small ice-cold hand!

Great fear came over me. I tried to pull back my arm, but the hand held on, and a sad voice cried: 'Let me in! Let me in!'

'Who are you?' I asked, while struggling to free myself.

'Catherine Linton,' it replied. (Why did I think of 'Linton'? I had read 'Earnshaw' twenty times, compared with 'Linton'.) 'I've come home. I'd lost my way on the moor.'

As it spoke, I saw, faintly, a child's face looking through the window.

'Let me in!' came the cry once more, while the hand continued to hold on to mine, almost maddening me with fear.

'How can I?' I said at last. 'Let me go, if you want me to let you in!'

The fingers loosened. I drew mine hurriedly through the hole, piled the books up against it, and closed my ears against the voice.

I seemed to keep them closed for over a quarter of an hour, but the moment I listened again, the sad cry was repeated.

Fear made me cruel.

'Go away!' I shouted. 'I'll never let you in, not if you beg for twenty years.'

'It is twenty years,' said the voice. 'Twenty years! I've been wandering for twenty years!'

The pile of books on my shelf moved as if they were being pushed forward. I tried to jump up, but could not, so I shouted aloud in fear.

Rapid footsteps hurried towards my door. Somebody pushed it open with a violent hand, and a light appeared. I sat up shivering.

In a half-whisper, clearly not expecting an answer, a voice said: 'Is anyone here?'

I pushed open the doors of my resting place. I shall not soon forget the effect that my action produced.

Heathcliff stood near the entrance, in his shirt and trousers, with a candle in his hand and his face as white as the wall behind him. My first movement affected him like an electric shock. The light fell from his hand.

'It's only your guest, sir,' I called out. 'I had the misfortune to cry out in my sleep, owing to a frightful dream.'

Heathcliff murmured a curse. He set the candle on a chair.

'And who showed you up to this room?' he asked.

'It was your servant, Zillah,' I replied. 'I suppose she wanted proof that there is a ghost. Well, there is!'

'What do you mean?' asked Heathcliff. 'Nothing could excuse the horrible noise you made, unless you were having your throat cut!'

'If that little ghost had got in at the window, she would probably have finished me!' I replied. 'As for Catherine Linton, or Earnshaw, or whatever she was called, she told me she had been walking the earth for twenty years now.'

I had hardly spoken these words, when I remembered the joining of Heathcliff's name with Catherine in the writing in the book.

'What do you mean by talking in this way to *me*?' thundered Heathcliff. 'How *dare* you, under my roof?'

I began to dress. Heathcliff sat down on the bed. I guessed by his irregular breathing that he was struggling against some powerful feeling.

'Mr Lockwood,' he said at last, 'you may go to my room. Your childish shouting has finished my chances of sleep for the night.'

'And mine too,' I replied. 'I'll walk in the yard until daylight, and then I'll be off.'

I left the room and then, not knowing the way, turned back to ask and saw, without intending to, the strange behaviour of my host.

He had got on to the bed and pulled open the window, bursting, as he did so, into a fit of uncontrollable weeping.

'Come in! Come in!' he cried. 'Cathy, do come! Oh, do, once more! Oh, my heart's dearest! Hear me this time, Catherine, at last!'

The spirit made no reply, but the snow and wind blew wildly in.

There was such suffering in this wild speech that I began to pity him. I went quietly down to the back kitchen, where I found the remains of a fire. Only half warm, I stretched myself on a wooden seat until morning, when I left as early as possible.

The air was clear, and cold as ice. Before I reached the bottom of the garden, my host came after me, and offered to go with me across the moor. I was glad that he did, as the whole hillside was one white ocean of snow, and the path was completely hidden.

We exchanged little conversation, and parted company at the entrance to Thrushcross Park. After losing myself among the trees, and sinking up to my neck in snow, I reached the Grange some time later, to a warm welcome from Mrs Dean, my housekeeper, who was beginning to believe that I had died on the moor.

Chapter 4   My Neighbours

By this time I was half frozen. I dragged myself upstairs, put on dry clothes, and sat in my sitting room, almost too weak to enjoy the cheerful fire and the hot coffee that the servant had prepared.

I had chosen this place, I remembered, for its loneliness. But how little we human beings know our own minds! Did I really want to live here?

By evening, I was already tired of my own company. I requested Mrs Dean, when she brought the supper, to sit down while I ate.

'You have lived here for some time,' I began.

'Eighteen years, sir. I came when the mistress was married, to help her. After she died, the master kept me as his housekeeper.'

'I'll turn the talk on my landlord's family,' I thought, 'and the pretty girl — I should like to know her history.'

With this intention, I asked why Heathcliff let Thrushcross Grange and preferred to live in a place so much less grand.

'Isn't he rich enough to keep the property in good order?' I inquired.

'Rich, sir!' she replied. 'Yes, he's rich enough to live in a finer house than this. But he's very careful with his money.'

'He had a son, it seems?'

'Yes, he had one. He is dead.'

'And the young lady, Mrs Heathcliff — where did she come from.'

'She is the daughter of my master, sir, who is now dead. Catherine Linton was her name before she married. I was her nurse, poor thing!'

'What! Catherine Linton!' I exclaimed. But a moment's thought told me that it was not my ghostly Catherine. 'And who is that Earnshaw, Hareton Earnshaw, who lives with Mr Heathcliff? Are they relations?'

'No. He is Mrs Linton's nephew, and the young lady's cousin. Hareton is the last of the Earnshaws, a very old family who owned Wuthering Heights, and Catherine is the only one left of the Lintons, whose family home was Thrushcross Grange. Have you been to the Wuthering Heights, sir? I should like to hear how she is.'

'Mrs Heathcliff? She looked very well, and very pretty, but not, I think, very happy.'

'Oh, well, I'm not surprised. And how did you like the master?'

'A rough man, Mrs Dean. Do you know anything of his history?'

'Everything, sir, except where he was born, and who his parents were, and how he first got his money. And Hareton has lost his rights! The unfortunate boy does not guess how he has been cheated of his property!'

'Well, Mrs Dean, I shall not rest if I go to bed. Be so good as to stay and tell me something about my neighbours.'

'Oh, certainly, sir! I'll just fetch a little sewing, and then I'll sit as long as you please.'

She hurried off, and I moved nearer to the fire. My head felt hot, and the rest of me felt cold. I was excited by the events of the last two days, and I began to fear that the effect on my health might be serious.

My fears proved to be true. The next weeks were spent in bed, and during my illness Mrs Dean often came to sit and keep me company.

While she sat, she told me, little by little, the story that follows.

PART 2   THE FIRST CATHERINE (1771–1784)

Told by Mrs Ellen (Nelly) Dean, housekeeper at Thrushcross Grange and formerly servant at Wuthering Heights

Chapter 5   The Unwanted Stranger

Wuthering Heights was built by the Earnshaws about 300 years ago, and until recently it remained the family home. Before I came to live at the Grange, I was almost always at the Heights, because when I was a baby my mother was nurse to Hindley Earnshaw, who was Hareton's father. As a child I often played with the children, Hindley and Catherine. I did little jobs, too, and helped on the farm when I was asked to.

One fine summer morning, Mr Earnshaw, the old master, came downstairs dressed for a journey. After he had told Joseph what had to be done during the day, he turned to his children and asked what he should bring them from the port of Liverpool. But, he said, it must be something small, as he intended to walk there and back, which was sixty miles each way. Hindley asked for a drum, and Cathy chose a whip; although she was hardly six years old, she could ride any horse on the farm. He then kissed his children goodbye and set out.

It seemed a long time to us all, the three days of his absence. Mrs Earnshaw expected him by supper time on the third evening, and she delayed the meal hour after hour but there was no sign of his coming. It became dark, and she would have sent the children to bed, but they begged sadly to stay up.

Just about eleven o'clock, the door opened and the master stepped in. He threw himself into a chair laughing and then he opened his big coat, which he held wrapped up in his arms.

'See here, wife! You must take this as a gift of God, though it's as dark as if it came from the devil.'

We crowded round, and over Catherine's head I had a view of a dirty, black-haired child in torn clothes. It was big enough both to walk and talk; in fact its face looked older than Catherine's. But when it was placed on its feet, it only stared around and repeated some sounds that nobody could understand. I was frightened, and Mrs Earnshaw was ready to throw it out of doors.

The master had seen it dying of hunger, and homeless, and unable to speak any English, in the streets of Liverpool. No one knew to whom it belonged. He was determined not to leave it so, his time and money being limited, he thought it better to take it straight home with him. I was told to wash it, give it clean clothes, and let it sleep with the children.

Hindley and Cathy were happy to look and listen, until they both began searching their father's pockets for the presents he had promised them. Hindley was a boy of fourteen, but when he took out what had been a drum, now broken to bits, he wept aloud; and Cathy, when she learned that the master had lost her whip in looking after the stranger, showed her temper by making ugly faces at the little thing, and received a blow from her father. They refused to have the child in their room, and so I put it outside on the stairs, hoping it might be gone in the morning. It crept to Mr Earnshaw's door, and there he found it. As a punishment for my unkindness I was sent out of the house.

On returning a few days later, I found they had called the child Heathcliff. It was the name of a son of the Earnshaws who had died in childhood, and it has served him ever since as both first and last name.

Miss Cathy and he were now very friendly, but Hindley hated him and the mistress never said a word when she saw him badly treated. He seemed a patient, unsmiling child used, perhaps, to unkindness, who would suffer Hindley's blows without complaint. When Mr Earnshaw discovered his son hitting the poor, fatherless child, as he called him, he was furious. He became strangely fond of Heathcliff, far more than of Catherine, who was too strong-willed and naughty to be a favourite.

From the beginning Heathcliff caused bad feeling, and by the time Mrs Earnshaw died two years later, the young master had learned to think of his father as hard and unkind, and of Heathcliff as the thief of his father's love.

I often asked myself what my master saw to admire so much in the unpleasant boy, who never, as far as I can remember, showed any signs of being grateful for the fond treatment he received.

I remember Mr Earnshaw once bought a pair of horses for the boys. Heathcliff took the finer one, but it soon hurt its foot. When he discovered this, he said to Hindley: 'You must exchange horses with me, or I'll tell your father of the three beatings you've given me this week.'

Hindley threatened him with an iron weight.

'Throw it,' said Heathcliff, 'and I'll tell how you said that you would turn me out of doors as soon as he died, and we'll see whether he won't turn you out immediately.'

Hindley threw it, hitting him on the chest, and knocking him over. He was up again at once, breathless and pale, and if I hadn't prevented it, he would have gone to the master and got full revenge.

'Take my horse, you dirty gypsy,' said young Hindley, 'and I pray he may break your neck!'

Heathcliff had gone to take possession of the animal, when Hindley finished his speech by knocking him over. I was surprised to see how calmly the child picked himself up. I persuaded him to let me lay the blame for the marks left by Hindley's blows on the horse, and he did not mind what story was told, since he had got what he wanted.

Chapter 6   Hindley Becomes Master

In the course of time, Mr Earnshaw's health began to fail. His strength left him suddenly, and he became easily annoyed. He got it into his head that because he liked Heathcliff, everyone hated the boy and wished to do him harm. It was a disadvantage to young Heathcliff, because as we didn't wish to upset the master, we all, except his son, gave in to him, and this was an encouragement to the boy's pride and black temper. Hindley's expressions of scorn moved his father to fury: Mr Earnshaw would seize his stick to strike him, and shake with anger at his own helplessness.

At last a friend of our employer, who earned some money by teaching the young Lintons and Earnshaws, advised that Hindley should be sent away to college, and Mr Earnshaw agreed, though with a heavy heart.

I hoped we would have peace now, and so we might have, except that Miss Cathy and Joseph were just as bad. Night after night the old servant had a string of complaints against Heathcliff and Cathy. As for Cathy, certainly she had ways such as I never saw in a child before. She put us out of patience fifty times and more in a day. From the hour she came downstairs until the hour she went to bed, we hadn't a minute's rest from her naughtiness. Her spirits were always high, her tongue was always going – singing, laughing, interrupting everybody. She was a wild, wicked young thing, but she had the prettiest eye and sweetest smile and lightest foot in our part of the country, and after all, I think she meant no harm. She was much too fond of Heathcliff. The greatest punishment we could invent for her was to keep her separated from him.

The hour came at last that ended Mr Earnshaw's troubles on earth. He died quietly in his chair one October evening.

Mr Hindley came home for the funeral and, a thing that set the neighbours whispering, he brought a wife. What she was, and where she was born, he never informed us. Probably she had neither money nor name, or he would never have kept his marriage secret from his father.

She was rather thin, but young and fresh, and her eyes were bright as diamonds. I did notice, it's true, that going upstairs made her breathe rather fast, and that she coughed rather badly sometimes.

Young Earnshaw had changed during the three years of his absence. He spoke and dressed quite differently. His wife expressed pleasure at having Cathy as a sister, kissed her, and gave her quantities of presents. Her love for her new sister didn't last very long, though, and a few words from her, mentioning a dislike for Heathcliff, were enough to stir up in her husband all his former hate for the boy. He drove him from their company to the servants, stopped his education, and made him work as hard as any other boy on the farm.

Heathcliff bore his treatment fairly well at first, because Cathy taught him all she learned and worked or played with him in the fields. They were both growing up quite wild and without manners, since the young master did not care how they behaved as long as they kept away from him.

One of their chief amusements was to run away to the moors in the morning and remain there all day. The punishment that followed was only something to be laughed at: they forgot everything the minute they were together again.

◆

One Sunday, it chanced that Catherine and Heathcliff were sent from the sitting room for making a noise. When I went to call them to supper, I couldn't find them anywhere. At last Hindley in a fury told us to lock the doors, and swore that nobody should let them in that night.

Everyone else went to bed, but I, too anxious to lie down, opened my window and put out my head to listen. After a time, I heard faint footsteps coming up the road. There was Heathcliff by himself.

'Where is Miss Catherine?' I cried. 'No accident, I hope?'

'At Thrushcross Grange,' he answered. 'Let me take off my wet clothes, and I'll tell you all about it.'

I urged him to take care not to wake the master. As he was undressing, he continued, 'Cathy and I escaped from the house to have an hour or two of freedom and, catching sight of the Grange lights, we thought we would just go and see how the Lintons passed their Sunday evenings. We ran from the top of the Heights to the Park without stopping – Catherine was completely beaten in the race, because she had no shoes on. You'll have to look for her shoes out there tomorrow. We crept through a broken fence and stood on a flowerbed under a window. By pulling ourselves up, we were able to see – ah! it was beautiful! – a lovely room, with chairs covered in red, and tables too, and a red floor, and a pure white ceiling bordered with gold, and little glass balls hanging in silver chains from the centre and shining with soft little lights. Edgar and his sister were there. Shouldn't they have been happy? And guess what they were doing! Isabella – I believe she is eleven – lay shouting at one end of the room. Edgar stood by the fire weeping, and in the middle of a table sat a little dog, which they had nearly pulled in two. That was their pleasure! We laughed at the spoilt things. Would you find me wishing to have what Catherine wanted? I'd not exchange my condition here for Edgar Linton's at Thrushcross Grange, not for a thousand lives!'

'Speak more quietly!' I interrupted. 'Still you haven't told me how Catherine was left behind.'

'I told you we laughed,' he answered. 'The Lintons heard us, and began to cry for their mother and father. We made horrible noises to frighten them even more, and then we dropped down from the edge of the window, because someone was coming outside. I had Cathy by the hand, and was urging her on, when suddenly she fell. They had let the watch-dog loose, and he had seized her leg. She didn't cry – no, she would not have done that. I got a stone and pushed it between the animal's jaws, but he held on. A servant came out. He got the dog off, and lifted Cathy up. She was sick, not from fear, I'm certain, but from pain.

'"What have you caught, Robert?" called Mr Linton.

'"A little girl, sir," he replied, "and there's a boy who looks like a thief," he added, catching hold of me. "Mr Linton, sir, keep your gun ready."

'He pulled me under the light, and Mrs Linton put her

glasses on and raised her hands in fear. The children crept nearer, and Isabella cried, "Lock him up, Papa. He's exactly like the son of the gypsy who stole my pet bird." Cathy now recovered from her faint. She heard the last speech and laughed. Edgar recognised her. They see us in church, you know.

'"That's Miss Earnshaw," he whispered to his mother.

'"Miss Earnshaw? Nonsense! Miss Earnshaw running about the country like a gypsy! But yes, surely it is — and her foot is bleeding."

'"What carelessness of her brother!" exclaimed Mr Linton, "to let her grow up like this! And where did she pick up this companion? A wicked boy, and quite unfit for a respectable house. Did you hear the language he was using?"

'I began cursing again, and so the servant was ordered to send me away. The curtain at the window was still partly open, and I stood to watch, because if Catherine had wished to return and they did not let her leave, I intended breaking the glass. She sat quietly on a comfortable chair. A servant brought a bowl of warm water and washed her feet. Mr Linton gave her a hot drink, and Isabella put a plateful of cakes on her knee. Afterwards, they dried and combed her beautiful hair and put her near the fire, and I left her cheerfully bringing a little life to the dull blue eyes of the Lintons. I saw they were full of stupid admiration. She is so completely superior to them, and to everybody else on earth — isn't she?'

'There will be trouble when Mr Hindley knows, Heathcliff,' I said.

My words came truer than I wished. Hindley was furious. The next day Mr Linton paid us a visit and talked to the young master about his responsibilities to his sister. As a result, Heathcliff was told that the next time he spoke to Catherine, he would be sent away.

Chapter 7   Catherine's Homecoming

Catherine stayed at Thrushcross Grange for five weeks, until Christmas. By that time her ankle was cured and her manners much improved. She had learned to enjoy fine clothes and admiration, so that instead of a wild, hatless, unmannered little thing jumping into the house and rushing up to us, a well-dressed little person, very careful of her appearance, climbed down from her horse. Hindley exclaimed with pleasure, 'Well, Cathy, you are quite a beauty! You look like a lady now.'

The dogs came running up to welcome her, but she hardly dared touch them for fear that they would spoil her beautiful dress. She kissed me carefully: I had flour on my clothes from making the Christmas cake. Then she looked round for Heathcliff.

He was hard to find at first. Since Cathy had been away, the treatment of him had been ten times worse than before. There was no one except me even to tell him to wash himself. His clothes had seen long service in mud and dust, his thick hair was uncombed, his face and hands needed soap and water. He had good reason to hide.

'Heathcliff, you may come forward,' cried Mr Hindley, enjoying his shame. 'You may come and wish Miss Catherine welcome, like all the other servants.'

Cathy flew to kiss her friend seven or eight times on his cheek, and then stopped, and stepping back, burst into a laugh, exclaiming, 'Why, how very dark and unpleasant you look! But that's because I'm used to Edgar and Isabella Linton.'

'Shake hands, Heathcliff,' ordered Hindley.

Shame and pride kept the boy immovable.

'I shall not,' he said at last. 'I shall not stand to be laughed at.'

He would have moved away from them, but Miss Cathy seized him.

'I didn't mean to laugh at you,' she said. 'It was only that you looked so strange. You're so dirty!'

She looked anxiously at her dress, fearing that he had marked it.

'You needn't have touched me,' he answered, following her eye. 'I shall be as dirty as I please.'

He rushed from the room, followed by the laughter of my master and mistress. Cathy was upset and could not understand his bad temper.

It was the evening before Christmas Day. Joseph had gone to pray. I sat alone in the kitchen, remembering my old master and his kindness to me. From these thoughts I passed to his fondness for Heathcliff and his fear that the boy would suffer after his death.

Catherine was in the sitting room with her brother and his wife, looking at the presents they had bought for her to give to the Lintons. I found Heathcliff in one of the farm buildings.

'Hurry, Heathcliff,' I said. 'Let me make you tidy before Miss Cathy comes out, and then you can sit together by the fire in the kitchen and have a long talk before bedtime.'

He went on with his work and never turned his head.

Cathy sat up late, preparing for her new friends, who were going to visit her the next day. She came into the kitchen once to speak to her old friend, but he was not there.

Chapter 8   An Unhappy Christmas

The next day Heathcliff rose early and took his bad temper on to the moors, not reappearing until the family had left for church.

By this time he seemed to be in a better state of mind. He stood near me for a time, and then finding his courage, said, 'Nelly, make me tidy. I'm going to be good.'

'It's time that you behaved,' I said. 'You have hurt Catherine's feelings. You are too proud. If you're ashamed, you must ask pardon. And though I have dinner to get ready, I'll make time to arrange you so that Edgar Linton shall look like a baby beside you. You are younger, but you're taller and twice as broad across the shoulders. You could knock him down in a second.'

Heathcliff's face brightened for a moment, then it darkened again.

'But Nelly, it wouldn't make him less good-looking. I wish I had light hair and a fair skin, and was as well dressed and rich as he!'

'And cried for his mother and sat at home all day if there is a little rain!' I added. 'Oh, Heathcliff, you are showing a poor spirit! Now, look in the glass and tell me if you don't find yourself rather good-looking too, now you're washed and combed and have finished with your bad temper. For all we know, your father was a king in some faraway country, and your mother a queen, and you were seized as a child by wicked sailors, and brought to England!'

So I continued to talk, and Heathcliff was beginning to look quite pleasant, when suddenly our conversation was interrupted by the sound of wheels moving up the road and entering the yard.

From the window we saw the two Lintons, covered with furs, climbing down from their horses. Catherine took each of the children by the hand and brought them into the house.

I urged my companion to go and show his good temper, but unfortunately for him, when he opened the door leading from the kitchen on one side, Hindley opened it on the other. They met, and the master, annoyed at seeing him clean and cheerful, or perhaps remembering Mr Linton's words, pushed him back sharply and ordered Joseph to send him upstairs until dinner was over.

'Away, you gypsy!' he cried. 'What! Are you trying to make

yourself look like your superiors! Wait till I get hold of that fine hair – see if I won't pull it a little longer!'

'It's long enough already,' remarked Edgar Linton from the doorway. 'It's like horse hair.'

Heathcliff's violent nature was not prepared to accept this insult. He seized a dish of hot apple pie and threw it right in the speaker's face. Edgar began to cry, and Isabella and Catherine hurried in. Mr Hindley dragged Heathcliff outside, while I got a kitchen cloth and rather unkindly rubbed Edgar's nose and mouth clean. Cathy stood by, confused and turning red with embarrassment.

'You shouldn't have spoken to him!' she said to Edgar. 'Now he'll be beaten, and I hate that! I can't eat my dinner.'

'I didn't speak to him,' wept the youth. 'I promised my mother I wouldn't say a word to him.'

'Well, don't cry,' said Catherine scornfully. 'You're not dead. My brother is coming. Be quiet!'

At the sight of all the food on the table, the little visitors recovered their good spirits. They were hungry after their journey, and no real harm had been done. I waited at the table behind the mistress's chair. Cathy lifted a mouthful, and then set it down again. Her cheeks were hot and the tears poured over them. She quickly dropped her fork and bent beneath the tablecloth to hide her feelings. She was unhappy all day.

In the evening we had a dance. Cathy begged that Heathcliff, who had been locked up by the master, might be freed, as Isabella had nobody to dance with; but Mr Hindley would not listen, and I had to fill the place. Our pleasure in the exercise was increased by the arrival of a band of fifteen musicians, and some singers too. Young Mrs Earnshaw loved the music, so they gave us plenty.

Catherine loved it too, but she said it sounded sweetest at the top of the stairs, and she went up in the dark. I followed. They shut the door below, never noticing our absence. She did not stop at the head of the stairs, but went on up the ladder to the top of the house, where Heathcliff was locked in, and spoke to him through the door.

When the singers had finished, I went to warn her. Instead of finding her outside, I heard her voice from inside. The naughty little thing had crept out through one small window in the roof, and along the outside and in through the window of Heathcliff's prison, and it was with the greatest difficulty that I could persuade her to come out again. When she did come, Heathcliff came with her.

I told them that I didn't mean to encourage their tricks, but as Heathcliff had not eaten at all since yesterday's dinner I would shut my eyes for once to his deceiving Mr Hindley. He went down, and I set him in a chair by the fire in the kitchen.

He was sick, and could eat little. He sat with his head in his hands. When I inquired what he was thinking about, he answered: 'I'm trying to decide how I shall take my revenge on Hindley. I don't care how long I wait, if only I can do it in the end.'

Chapter 9   'No Company At All'

On the morning of a bright day in the following June, 1778, Hareton, the last of the ancient family of Earnshaw, was born. He was a fine boy. The doctor said, though, that his mother had had a sickness of the lungs for many months and would not live long. Mr Hindley refused to believe it, but one night, while she was leaning on his shoulder, a fit of coughing seized her. He raised her in his arms; she put hers around his neck, her face changed, and she was dead.

The child, Hareton, was left completely in my charge. His father, so long as he saw him healthy and never heard him cry, was happy. He had room in his heart for only his wife and himself, and he could not bear the loss. He neither wept nor prayed; he cursed God and man, and gave himself up to wild living. The servants all left: Joseph and I were the only two who would stay. Cathy's teacher stopped visiting us, and nobody respectable came near us except Edgar Linton, who came to see Cathy.

At fifteen she was the queen of our part of the country: a proud, strong-willed girl, but completely dependable and loyal. Heathcliff still had his place in her heart and Linton, with all his superiority, found it difficult to awaken equally strong feelings.

Catherine did not show her rough side in the Lintons' company, but had the good sense to be ashamed of being rude where she was received with such unfailing good manners. The old lady and gentleman were deceived by her pretty ways, and became fond of her, and she gained the admiration of Isabella and the heart and soul of her brother.

One afternoon, Mr Hindley had gone out, so Heathcliff had given himself a holiday. He had reached about the age of sixteen and had by that time lost the advantage of his early education. His childhood sense of superiority, developed by the love that old Mr Earnshaw felt for him, had disappeared. He had struggled for a long time to keep up with Catherine in her studies but had given up. Then his appearance began to show his state of mind. His walk lacked confidence, he looked unpleasant and rarely spoke, and he took pleasure in stirring up the dislike of those whom he met.

Catherine and he were still loyal companions when his work was done, and on this occasion he came into the house in search of her. I was helping her to arrange her dress, as she thought she had the whole place to herself and had let Edgar Linton know of her brother's absence.

'Why have you got that silk dress on?' asked Heathcliff. 'Nobody is coming here, I hope?'

'Not that I know of,' replied Catherine rather awkwardly, 'but you should be in the fields now, Heathcliff.'

'Hindley doesn't often free us of his presence,' remarked the boy. 'I'll not work any more today. I'll stay with you.'

He moved towards the fire. Catherine looked at him uncertainly.

'Isabella and Edgar Linton talked of calling this afternoon,' she said, after a short silence. 'As it's raining, I don't really expect them, but they may come.'

'Order Ellen to say that you are out, Cathy,' he went on. 'Don't turn me out for those miserable, silly friends of yours.'

'And should I always be sitting with you?' she demanded. 'What good do I get? You might be a baby, unable to talk, for anything you say to amuse me!'

'You never told me before that I talked too little, or that you disliked my company, Cathy!' exclaimed Heathcliff, greatly upset.

'It's no company at all, when people know nothing, and say nothing,' she complained.

Her companion rose, but he had no time to express his feelings further, because a horse's feet were heard on the stone path outside, and after a gentle knock young Linton entered, his fair, good-looking face shining with pleasure. No doubt Cathy noticed the difference between her friends, as the one came in and the other left.

'I've not come too soon, have I?' said Edgar, giving me a look.

'No,' answered Catherine. 'What are you doing here, Nelly?'

'My work, miss,' I replied. Mr Hindley had given me orders to be present at any private visits young Linton chose to pay.

She stepped up behind me and whispered: 'Take yourself and your work off!'

'It's a good opportunity, now that the master is away,' I answered loudly. 'He hates me to do this tidying when he is in the room. I'm sure Mr Edgar will excuse me.'

She, thinking that Edgar could not see her, pulled the cloth from my hand and hit me very sharply on the arm. She hurt me, and besides, I enjoyed punishing her pride, so I got up and cried out: 'Oh, Miss Cathy, that's a nasty trick! You've no right to hit me.'

'I didn't touch you, you lying thing!' she exclaimed, her fingers ready to repeat the act, and her ears red with fury.

'What's this, then?' I replied, showing the mark on my arm.

She struck the ground with her foot; then, driven by the naughty spirit within her, hit me on the cheek, a blow that filled both my eyes with tears.

'Catherine! Catherine!' exclaimed Edgar, deeply upset by the double fault of lying and violence.

Little Hareton, who followed me everywhere and was sitting near me on the floor, began crying and talking of 'wicked Aunt Cathy', which turned her fury against him. She seized his shoulders and shook him until he became pale and Edgar, without thinking, took hold of her hands to free him. In a moment one hand was pulled from his, and the surprised young man felt it on his own ear in a way that could not be mistaken for a joke.

The insulted visitor moved to the place where he had put down his hat, pale and with a trembling lip.

'Where are you going?' demanded Catherine, moving to the door.

'Can I stay after you have struck me?' asked Edgar.

Catherine was silent.

'You've made me afraid and ashamed of you,' he continued. 'I'll not come here again.'

Catherine's tears began to fall.

'And you told an untruth,' he said.

'Well, go, if you please! Get away! And now I'll cry — I'll cry until I'm sick!'

She dropped down on her knees by a chair.

Edgar walked out into the yard, and then he looked back through the window. He possessed the power to go away as much as a cat possesses the power to leave a mouse half killed, or a bird half eaten. He turned and hurried into the house again and shut the door.

When I went in later to inform them that Earnshaw had come home furiously drunk, I saw that the quarrel had simply brought them closer and helped them to put off the appearance of friendship and admit to being lovers.

Chapter 10   Cathy's Choice

My warning of Mr Hindley's arrival drove Edgar to his horse and Catherine to her room. I hurried to hide Hareton, and to take the shot out of the master's gun for fear that in his excited condition he would do harm.

Earnshaw entered, murmuring terrible curses, and caught me just as I was putting his son out of sight. He picked up the boy, who was shouting and kicking, as the child had an equal terror of his fondness and of his fury. The drunken father carried him upstairs, and paused unsteadily, looking down, as I begged him to take care. Still struggling in his father's arms, Hareton managed to free himself and fell.

At that exact moment Heathcliff arrived below and, by a natural movement, caught the child and set him on his feet. His face became dark with anger when he looked up and realized that he had missed an excellent opportunity for revenge.

Earnshaw came slowly down, a little ashamed.

'It's your fault,' he said to me. 'You should have kept him out of sight. Is he hurt?'

'Hurt!' I cried angrily. 'I am surprised that his mother

doesn't rise from her grave to see how you treat him!'

He took a bottle of wine and poured some into a glass, impatiently ordering us to go.

I carried the child into the kitchen, and sat down to calm him. Heathcliff, as I thought, walked out into the yard. I found out afterwards that he only got as far as the other side of the high-backed kitchen seat, behind which he sat unseen.

I was nursing Hareton on my knee, when Cathy put her head in at the door and whispered: 'Are you alone, Nelly?'

'Yes, miss.'

'Where's Heathcliff?'

'Doing his work outside.'

He did not call out that this was not so. Perhaps he was half asleep.

A long pause followed. A tear fell from Catherine's cheek.

'Oh!' she cried at last. 'I'm very unhappy!'

'That's a pity,' I replied. 'You're hard to please: so many friends and so few cares, and you can't make yourself happy.'

'Nelly, will you keep a secret?' She knelt down beside me. 'I want to know what I should do. Today Edgar Linton has asked me to marry him. I accepted him. Say whether I was wrong.'

'Do you love him?'

'Who can help it? Of course I do.'

'Why do you love him, Miss Cathy?'

'Well, because he's very good-looking, and pleasant to be with.'

'That's bad.'

'He'll be rich, and I shall like to be the greatest woman in the area.'

'Then why are you unhappy? Your brother will be pleased. The old lady and gentleman won't object, I think. You will escape from a disorderly, comfortless home into a wealthy, respectable one. Where is the difficulty?'

'Here – and here!' replied Catherine, putting one hand on her forehead and the other on her breast. 'In whichever place the soul lives. In my soul and in my heart, I'm certain I'm wrong.'

She seated herself by me. Her face became sadder; her hands trembled.

'I have no right to marry Edgar Linton, and if that wicked brother of mine had not brought Heathcliff to such a low state, I wouldn't have thought of it. It would degrade me to marry Heathcliff now, so he shall never know how I love him – and that, not because he's good-looking, Nelly, but because he's more myself than I am.'

I heard a slight movement before the speech ended. I turned my head and saw Heathcliff rise from a seat and creep out. He had listened until he heard Catherine say it would degrade her to marry him.

I urged my companion to speak lower.

'Why?' she asked, looking round nervously.

'Joseph is here,' I answered, 'and I think that Heathcliff is about at this moment.'

'Oh, he couldn't have heard me!' she said. 'Give me Hareton while you get the supper, and let me have it with you. I will feel much more comfortable if I can persuade myself that Heathcliff has no idea of my feelings. He hasn't, has he? He doesn't know what being in love is?'

'I see no reason why he shouldn't know as well as you,' I answered, 'and if you are his choice, he is the most unfortunate being that ever was born! As soon as you become Mrs Linton, he loses friend and love and all! Have you considered how you'll bear the separation, and how he'll bear to be left quite friendless in the world?'

'He left friendless! We separated! Not as long as I live! Edgar must get rid of his dislike of him. Nelly, did it never strike you that if Heathcliff and I married, we would have nothing, but if I marry Edgar I can help Heathcliff to rise in life, and place him out of my brother's power?'

'With your husband's money? That's the worst reason you've given for being the wife of young Linton.'

'It's not! It's the best! This is for one who ... I can't express it; but surely you and everybody have an idea that there is or should be an existence of yours beyond you? My great miseries in this world have been Heathcliff's miseries: my life is his. If everything else were destroyed, and he remained, I should still continue to be; and if everything else remained, and he were gone, the universe would seem a stranger. My love for Edgar is like the leaves in the woods: time will change it, as the winter changes the trees. My love for Heathcliff is like the unchanging rocks beneath: a cause of little conscious pleasure, but necessary to my being. Nelly, I am Heathcliff! He's always in my mind, as part of me.'

'If I can make any sense of your nonsense, miss, it only causes me to believe that either you know nothing of the duties that you take on yourself in marrying, or else you are a wicked girl.'

The entrance of Joseph put an end to our talk.

Hours passed by, and there was no sign of Heathcliff. Catherine became worried, especially when I told her that he had really heard a large part of what she had said.

'Where do you think he is? What did I say? I've forgotten. Was he upset by my bad temper this afternoon? I do wish he'd come.'

It was a very dark evening for summer, and at about midnight, while we were still sitting up, a storm came over the Heights. There was a violent wind, as well as thunder and lightning, and either one or the other split a tree and knocked down a part of the east chimney.

Catherine remained out by the gate, waiting for Heathcliff, listening and calling, careless of the weather, until she was wet to the skin. She refused to take off her wet things, and in the morning I found her still seated near the fireplace. She was shivering uncontrollably, and Hindley ordered me to get her to bed.

I shall never forget the scene when we reached her room. It frightened me. I thought she was going mad, and I begged Joseph to run for the doctor. It was the beginning of high fever. The doctor declared her to be dangerously ill, told me to feed her on liquids and to take care that she did not throw herself from the window. He then left, as he had enough to do in the area, where the houses were often widely separated.

I was not a gentle nurse and Joseph and the master were no better. Cathy was as tiring and as difficult to manage as any sick person can be. Old Mrs Linton paid us several visits and, when Catherine was recovering, took her to Thrushcross Grange. The poor lady had reason to be sorry for her kindness. She and her husband both caught the fever and died within a few days of each other.

Our young lady returned to us prouder and more violent in temper than ever. Heathcliff had never been heard of since the thunderstorm, and one day I had the misfortune to lay the blame for his disappearance on her, where in fact it belonged. For several months she would not speak to me, except as a servant. She considered herself to be a woman now, and our mistress, and thought her recent illness gave her a special claim to attention. The doctor had said that she could not bear people going much against her wishes, and ought to have her own way, so no one dared disobey her. Her brother was worried by the threat of some kind of fit that often attacked her during her fury; he allowed her whatever she pleased, in order to avoid awakening her fierce temper.

Three years after his father's death, Edgar Linton led her to church and married her, believing himself the happiest man alive.

Chapter 11　The Return

Much against my wishes, I was persuaded to leave Wuthering Heights and go with Cathy to her new home. Little Hareton was nearly five years old and I had just begun to teach him his letters. We parted sadly.

When she was at Thrushcross Grange, Catherine behaved much better than I had dared to expect. She seemed almost too fond of Edgar, and even to his sister she showed plenty of love. I noticed that Mr Edgar had a fear of causing her the least displeasure. In order not to cause grief to a kind master I learned to be more careful with my tongue, and for the space of half a year the gunpowder lay harmless as sand because no fire came near to explode it. Catherine had days of low spirits now and then, which her husband respected as the result of her former illness, but I believe they were really in possession of deep and growing happiness.

It ended.

On a golden evening in September I was coming from the garden with a basket of apples that I had been collecting. It was half dark, and the moon looked over the high wall of the yard, making strange shadows in the corners of the building.

My eyes were on the moon, when I heard a voice behind me say: 'Nelly, is that you?'

It was a deep voice, and foreign in sound, but something in the manner of pronouncing my name made it familiar. Somebody moved near the door of the house, and as I came nearer I saw more clearly a tall man dressed in dark clothes.

'Who can it be?' I thought.

A beam of light fell on his face. The cheeks were pale, and half covered with black hair; the forehead was heavy, the eyes deep-set and strange. I recognized the eyes.

'What!' I cried. 'You've come back? Is it really you?'

'Yes, it's Heathcliff,' he replied, looking from me up at the windows. 'Are they at home? Where is she? Speak! I want to have one word with her – with your mistress. Go, and say that some person from Gimmerton village desires to see her.'

'How will she take it? How changed you are! Have you been a soldier?'

'Go and carry my message,' he interrupted. 'I'm in a state of misery until you do!'

When I got to the sitting room, Mr and Mrs Linton were sitting together at a window looking out at the trees. Everything looked peaceful, and I could not persuade myself to speak.

I was actually going away leaving the words unsaid, when a sense of my own foolishness forced me to return and give the message.

'Close the curtains, Nelly, and bring up tea. I'll be back again soon.'

She left the room, and Edgar inquired carelessly who it was.

'Someone that mistress does not expect. That Heathcliff, sir, who used to live at Mr Earnshaw's.'

'What! The gypsy – the farm boy?'

'Take care! You must not call him by those names, master. She was nearly heartbroken when he ran off.'

Shortly after, Catherine flew upstairs, wild and breathless.

'Oh, Edgar, Edgar,' she exclaimed, throwing her arms round his neck, 'Heathcliff's come back!'

'Well, well,' cried her husband, sounding displeased, 'there's no need to be so excited, surely!'

'I know you didn't like him,' she answered, controlling her pleasure a little, 'but, for me, you must be friends now. Shall I tell him to come up?'

'Here?' he said. 'Wouldn't the kitchen be a more suitable place?'

Mrs Linton looked at him. 'No,' she replied, half angry, half amused, 'I can't sit in the kitchen.'

She was about to run off again, but Edgar stopped her.

'You ask him to step up,' he said, addressing me. 'Catherine, the whole household need not witness the sight of your welcoming a runaway servant as a brother.'

Heathcliff followed me up without further speech, and I brought him into the presence of the master and mistress, whose red cheeks showed signs of heated argument. The lady ran forward, took his hands, and led him to Linton; then she seized Linton's fingers and pressed them into his.

Now clearly shown up by the fire and candlelight, the change in Heathcliff surprised me more than ever. He had grown into a tall, active, well-formed man, beside whom my master seemed only a youth. His upright appearance suggested that he had been in the army. His face was older in expression and firmer in shape; it looked intelligent, and had lost all former marks of degradation. A fierceness lay hidden in the eyes, but his manner was serious, even gentlemanly, and quite without roughness. My master's surprise equalled or went beyond mine, and for a minute he was puzzled as to how to receive the farm boy, as he called him.

'Sit down, sir,' he said at last. 'It is Mrs Linton's wish that you should be welcomed here, and of course I am happy to give her pleasure.'

'And I also,' answered Heathcliff. 'I shall be pleased to stay an hour or two.'

He took a seat opposite Catherine, who kept her eyes fixed on him. He did not raise his eyes to her often, but each time they expressed more confidently the pure pleasure he felt in her presence.

'I shall think it a dream tomorrow,' cried Catherine. 'But, cruel Heathcliff, you don't deserve this welcome. To be absent and silent for three years, and never think of me!'

'A little more than you have thought of me,' he replied.

'I heard of your marriage, Cathy, not long ago, and I planned to have just one quick look at you, take my revenge on Hindley, and then put an end to my own life. Your welcome has put such ideas out of my head. I've fought through a bitter life since I last heard your voice, and you must forgive me, because I struggled only for you!'

'Catherine, unless we are to have cold tea, please come to the table,' interrupted Linton, trying to speak in his ordinary voice but pale with annoyance.

Catherine took up her post, and Miss Isabella came in. The meal was over in a few minutes. Catherine's cup was never filled: she could neither eat nor drink. Edgar hardly swallowed a mouthful.

Their guest did not stay more than an hour longer. I asked, as he left, if he was going to Gimmerton.

'No, to Wuthering Heights,' he answered. 'I called this morning, expecting you would still be there, Nelly, and could give me news of Catherine. There were some persons there sitting at cards, whom I joined and, finding I have plenty of money now, Hindley invited me to repeat my visit. I shall try to stay there, so I can be within walking distance of Catherine. Hindley is greedy, and I shall pay him well.'

Mr Earnshaw invited him! I had a feeling in my heart that Heathcliff should have remained away.

Chapter 12   Miss Isabella

Heathcliff – Mr Heathcliff, I should say in future – used his freedom to visit Thrushcross Grange only occasionally at first. Catherine also judged it wise not to show too much pleasure in receiving him. My master's anxiety died down and, for a time, turned in another direction.

The new cause of trouble came from an unexpected misfortune. Isabella Linton suddenly developed strong feelings for the visitor. She was now a young lady of eighteen, childish in her manners though possessing a quick understanding and a quick temper, too, if annoyed. Her brother loved her dearly and, besides the shame of a marriage with a man of unknown origin, he had the sense to see that Heathcliff's nature was unchangeable, even if his outer appearance had improved.

We had all noticed for some time that Miss Linton was pale and unhappy and hard to please, and we had excused her in some degree because her health was weak. One day, when she had been particularly difficult, Mrs Linton threatened to send for the doctor. Isabella at once exclaimed that her health was perfect, and that it was only Cathy's unkindness that made her unhappy.

'How can you say I am unkind?' cried the mistress, surprised. 'When have I been unkind? Tell me.'

'Yesterday,' replied Isabella, weeping.

'Yesterday? On what occasion?'

'In our walk on the moor. You told me to wander where I pleased, while you went on with Mr Heathcliff.'

'And that's your idea of unkindness?' said Catherine laughing.

'You wished me away, because I wanted to be with . . .'

'Well?' said Catherine, seeing her pause.

'With him, and I won't always be sent off! You are a selfish thing, Cathy, and want no one to be loved but yourself.'

'I hope I have misunderstood you, Isabella?'

'No, you have not. I love him more than you ever loved Edgar; and he might love me, if you would let him!'

'I wouldn't like to be you at all, then!' declared Catherine. 'It's only because you haven't the least idea of his real nature that you can allow such a dream to enter your head. Don't imagine that he's got a heart of gold: he's a fierce, pitiless, cruel man. I know he couldn't love a Linton, but he might be ready to marry you for your money. There's my picture of him, and I'm his friend.'

'For shame! For shame!' cried Isabella. 'You're worse than twenty enemies, you poisonous friend!'

'Put him out of your thoughts, Miss Isabella,' I said. 'Mrs Linton spoke strongly, but I can't say that she's wrong. She has greater knowledge of his heart than anyone else. Honest people don't hide what they have done. How has he been living? How has he got rich? Why is he staying at Wuthering Heights, with a man whom he hates? They say Mr Hindley is worse since he came. They sit up all night playing cards and drinking, and Hindley has been borrowing money to pay his debts.'

'You're as bad as the rest, Ellen,' she replied. 'I shan't listen to your stories.'

The next day my master had to go to a neighbouring town on business and Heathcliff, knowing of his absence, called rather earlier than usual. Catherine and Isabella were sitting in the library, unfriendly and silent. The younger lady was worried by her own recent foolishness in revealing her secret feelings, and Catherine was really offended and ready to punish her companion. As she saw Heathcliff pass the window, she smiled to herself. Isabella, her head in a book, remained unconscious of the visitor until the door opened and it was too late to escape.

'Come in!' exclaimed the mistress brightly, pulling a chair to the fire. 'You're just the person we would both of us choose for our companion. Heathcliff, I'm proud to show you somebody who is fonder of you than myself. Poor little Isabella is breaking her heart for you! No, no, Isabella, you shan't run off,' she continued, taking a firm hold of the girl's wrist.

Heathcliff showed no sign of interest, and Isabella whispered an urgent request to be set free.

'Certainly not!' cried Mrs Linton. 'I won't be called a selfish thing again. Heathcliff, why don't you look pleased?'

Heathcliff looked hard at Isabella. 'I think you are mistaken,' he

41

said. 'She wishes to be out of my society now, in any case.'

The poor girl could not bear it. Her face became white and then red. Catherine still refused to let her go, until she began to use her nails.

'What did you mean by treating the poor thing in that way, Cathy?' Heathcliff asked, when the door had closed after her. 'You weren't speaking the truth, were you?'

'I promise you I was,' she replied.

'All her brother's possessions will one day be hers, won't they?' he asked, after a short pause.

'Not if I bear a son,' answered his companion. 'Forget this matter. You're too fond of thinking of other people's possessions.'

They did dismiss the subject from conversation, but I saw Heathcliff smile in a most unpleasant way when Mrs Linton was out of the room.

Chapter 13   An Evil Influence

Mr Heathcliff's visits worried me as much as they did my master, and his long stay at the Heights was a mystery with no solution. Sometimes I thought I would go and see how everything was at the farm, but then I remembered Mr Hindley's hopelessly bad habits, and I decided not to re-enter that unhappy house.

One time I passed near the farm on a journey to Gimmerton. It was a bright autumn afternoon, but the sunshine reminded me of summer, and I came to the stone marking the way across the moor. It was a favourite place of mine, a place loved by Hindley and myself twenty years before. Bending down I saw at the bottom of the rock a hole, where we used to keep our little toys, still now full of shells and smooth stones; and then it seemed that I saw my former childhood friend seated on the grass.

The child lifted its face and stared straight into mine. It

disappeared at once, but it was waiting for me when I reached the gate of the Heights, and further thought suggested that this must be Hareton, my Hareton, not changed greatly since I left him ten months before.

'My little dear!' I cried, forgetting my foolish fears. 'Hareton, it's Nelly, your nurse.'

He moved back, and picked up a large stone. He didn't recognize me. I began to speak, but the stone struck my head, and the little boy shouted a string of curses, twisting his baby face into an evil expression that shocked me. Ready to weep, I took an orange from my pocket and offered it. He paused, and then seized it from my hand.

'Who taught you those fine words, my child?' I asked.

He swore at me. I offered another orange, but kept it out of reach.

'Tell me where you get lessons, and you shall have it. Who's your master?'

'My father.'

'And what do you learn from him?'

'Nothing,' he said, 'but to keep out of his way. He can't bear me because I swear at him.'

'And who teaches you to swear?'

'Heathcliff.'

I asked whether he liked Heathcliff.

'Yes.'

I tried to find out the reason. I could only understand the sentences, 'I don't know; he punishes my father for what he does to me – he curses him. He says I must do as I like.'

'And don't you have a teacher to show you how to read and write, then?' I continued.

'No. There was one, but Heathcliff promised to knock his teeth out if he came again.'

I put the orange into his hand and told him to let his father know that a woman called Nelly Dean was waiting to speak to him. He entered the house but, instead of Hindley, Heathcliff appeared at the door, and I turned and ran down the road, as frightened as if I had seen an evil spirit.

Chapter 14   The Quarrel

The next time Heathcliff came, my young lady chanced to be feeding some birds in the courtyard. He was not in the habit of showing her any special attention but this time, as soon as he saw her, he looked carefully up at the front of the house. I remained hidden behind the kitchen window.

He stepped across to Isabella, and said something. She seemed anxious to get away, but to prevent it he laid his hand on her arm. She turned her face away. With another quick look up at the house, and supposing himself to be unseen, he put his arms around her.

'For shame!' I cried.

'Who is it, Nelly?' said Catherine's voice behind me.

'Your worthless friend!' I replied. 'What excuse do you think he will find for making love to Miss Isabella, when he told you he hated her?'

Mrs Linton saw Isabella struggle to free herself and run into the garden. A minute later, Heathcliff opened the door.

'Heathcliff, what are you doing? I said you must let her alone!'

'What is it to you?' he answered roughly. 'I have a right to kiss her, if she chooses. I'm not your husband: you needn't be jealous of me. And, Catherine, I have a few plain words to say to you now. I want you to understand that you have treated me shamefully! Do you hear? And if you think I'll suffer unrevenged, you are mistaken. For now, though, thank you for telling me Isabella's secret. I'll make good use of it.'

'What new side to his character is this?' exclaimed Mrs Linton.

'I have no wish to take revenge on you,' continued Heathcliff less violently. 'You are welcome to play with me until my death for your amusement, only allow me to amuse myself a little in the same way. Having ruined my life, don't expect me to be good!'

'Oh, you want to make people suffer, do you!' cried Catherine. 'You prove it! Edgar has just got back his good temper, and I begin to feel safe and comfortable, so you are determined to start a quarrel. Quarrel with Edgar, if you please, and deceive his sister; you'll have chosen just the best way to revenge yourself on me.'

The conversation ended.

Catherine sat by the fire, disturbed and unhappy. Her temper was getting beyond her control. Heathcliff stood with folded arms, thinking dark thoughts. In this position I left them to look for the master.

'The mistress is in the kitchen, sir,' I said. 'She's very upset by Mr Heathcliff's behaviour.' And I told him as much as I dared of what had happened.

'I won't bear this!' he declared. 'Call me two men from the servants' hall, Ellen.'

He went downstairs and, followed by me, entered the kitchen. Catherine and Heathcliff had returned to their quarrel. On seeing him, they became silent.

'I have been patient with you until now, sir,' said Linton to Heathcliff. 'I have foolishly allowed you here, because Catherine wished to keep up the connection. Your presence is a moral poison that would harm the purest. For that reason, and to prevent further evil, I demand that you leave this house immediately, and for the last time.'

Heathcliff looked scornfully at him.

'Cathy, this lamb of yours threatens like a lion!' he said.

My master signalled to me to fetch the men. Mrs Linton

pulled me back and locked the inner door.

'Fair means!' she said to her husband. 'If you haven't the courage to attack him yourself, say you are sorry, or allow yourself to be beaten.'

Mr Linton tried to seize the key from her, but she threw it into the hottest part of the fire. He was attacked by a nervous trembling and became as pale as death.

'I wish you joy of him, Cathy!' said her friend. 'And that is the weak-kneed thing that you preferred to me! Is he weeping, or is he going to faint with fear?'

He gave the chair on which Linton was leaning a push. My master jumped up and struck him on the throat. It took away Heathcliff's breath for a minute. Linton walked out of the back door into the yard, and from there to the front entrance.

'There, you can't come here again now,' cried Catherine. 'Get away. He'll return with guns. You've played an evil trick on me, Heathcliff!'

'Do you suppose I'm going, with that blow to answer?'

Two of the gardeners, with Linton, had already entered the yard. Heathcliff, on further thought, decided to avoid a struggle against three servants. He broke the lock of the inner door and made his escape.

Mrs Linton, who was by now very much excited, told me to go upstairs with her.

'I'm nearly mad, Nelly,' she exclaimed. 'My head is bursting. Tell Isabella to avoid me. She is the cause of all this, and if anyone makes me angrier at present I shall become wild. And, Nelly, if you see Edgar again tonight, tell him I'm in danger of being seriously ill. I hope I shall be, because I want to frighten him. Besides, he might come and begin a string of complaints. I'm certain I should answer back, and God knows where we should end! You know that I am in no way to blame in this matter. Well, if I can't keep Heathcliff as my friend – if Edgar will be jealous and selfish — I'll try to break their hearts by breaking my own. Nelly, I wish you would look rather more anxious about me.

I thought privately that she could have managed to control herself, and I did not wish to frighten her husband. I therefore said nothing when I saw him coming upstairs.

'I shall not stay, Catherine,' he said, without any anger in his voice. 'I have only one question to ask: will you give up Heathcliff, or will you give me up?'

'Oh, heavens!' interrupted the mistress. 'Let us hear no more of it now! Your cold blood can't be worked into a fever, but mine can!'

'To get rid of me, answer my question,' went on Mr Linton. 'You must answer it, and your violence does not frighten me. You can be as calm as anyone when you please.'

'I demand to be left alone,' exclaimed Catherine furiously. 'Don't you see that I can hardly stand? Leave me!'

She rang the bell until it broke. I had been waiting outside, but I did not hurry to enter. Her fury was enough to make the calmest person lose their temper. There she lay, striking her head against the arm of a chair. Mr Linton stood looking at her, and told me to fetch some water.

She would not drink, so I shook some drops on her face. In a few seconds she stretched herself out stiff, while her cheeks became pale as death. Linton looked worried.

'There is nothing the matter,' I whispered. I didn't want him to give in, though I too was afraid. I told him how she had wished to frighten him by one of her fits. She was well enough to hear and understand me, because she jumped up, her eyes flashing, and rushed from the room. The master directed me to follow, but she locked herself in her bedroom, where she remained for the next three days refusing all offers of food.

As for Mr Linton, he spent his time in the library. He had an hour's private talk with Miss Isabella, in which he warned her that if she were mad enough to encourage Heathcliff, it would end all ties between them as brother and sister.

Chapter 15   Illness

Miss Linton wandered round the park, always silent and almost always in tears. Her brother shut himself up among books that he never opened, in the faint but continuing hope that Catherine would ask his pardon for her behaviour. She went on refusing food, with the idea that her absence from the meal table would bring Edgar to her feet. I went on with my duties as usual, believing that I was the only sensible person in the house.

At last, on the third day, or rather, late in the evening, Mrs Linton, looking pale and tired, unlocked her door, and asked for food and water as she believed she was dying. I brought her tea and bread and butter.

'What is that dull being doing?' she demanded.

'If you mean Mr Linton,' I replied, 'he's fairly well. He is continually among his books.'

I would not have spoken so if I had known her true condition, but I could not get rid of the idea that she was acting a part of her illness.

'Among his books!' she cried. 'And I am near the grave! Oh, does he know how changed I am?' She stared at her face in a mirror hanging on the opposite wall.

'If I were sure it would kill him,' she went on, 'I'd kill myself now.'

She could not bear the thought that I had put into her head, of Edgar's quiet lack of interest. Throwing herself from side to side, she became feverish; then, raising herself up, burning with heat, she demanded that I should open the window. It was the middle of the winter, and I objected. The expression on her face began to worry me terribly. It reminded me of her former illness, and of the doctor's warning that no one should go against her wishes. She had even torn the bedclothes with her teeth.

'Lie down and shut your eyes,' I said. 'A sleep would do you good.'

'Oh, I wish I were a girl again! If only I were in my bed in my old home!' she cried. 'And the wind sounding through the trees near the window! Do let me feel it – it comes straight from the moor!'

To please her, I held the window open for a few seconds. An icy wind rushed through. I closed the window again.

'How long is it since I shut myself up here?' she asked suddenly.

'Four nights and three days,' I replied. 'Long enough to live on cold water and bad temper.'

'It seems a great many hours. I remember being in the sitting room after they had quarrelled, and running upstairs. As soon as I locked the door, complete blackness came over me. I couldn't explain to Edgar how certain I felt of having a fit if he went on annoying me. Open the window wide again,' she commanded. 'You won't give me a chance of life. Very well, I'll do it myself.'

Before I could stop her, she crossed the room unsteadily and threw open the window, careless of the air, which cut like a knife. I begged, and at last tried to force her back to bed, but her feverish strength resisted mine.

I was planning how to reach something to wrap around her, without letting go my hold of her, when Mr Linton entered.

'Oh, sir!' I cried, making signs to him to keep back the exclamation that rose to his lips at the sight that met him. 'My poor mistress is ill, and I can't manage her at all. Please, come and persuade her to go to bed.'

'Catherine ill!' he said, hurrying to us. 'Shut the window, Ellen!'

He was silent, worried by the change in Mrs Linton's appearance. I murmured something about not having known of her condition before, but I felt that I gave my explanations awkwardly. My master looked displeased and took his wife in his arms. At first she made no sign of recognition, but by degrees she fixed her attention on him.

'Ah! You've come, have you, Edgar Linton,' she said in an angry voice. 'You are one of the things that are never found when they are wanted. You'll be sorry when I'm in my grave, where I'm going before spring is over!'

'Catherine! Am I nothing to you any more? Do you love that miserable Heath—'

'If you mention that name, I'll end the matter by a jump from this window! Return to your books. I don't want you now.'

'Her mind wanders, sir,' I said. 'She has been talking nonsense the whole evening. We must be careful not to annoy her.'

'I want no further advice from you,' answered Mr Linton. 'You knew your mistress's nature, and you encouraged me to go against her. And not to give me any idea of how she has been all these three days! It was heartless!'

I began to defend myself, thinking it too bad to be blamed for the faults of another. Then, determined to go for medical help on my own responsibility, I left the room.

In passing through the garden, I saw something white hanging from a hook fixed into the wall. It was Miss Isabella's little dog, tied with a handkerchief and nearly at its last breath. While untying the animal, it seemed to me that I heard the sound of horses' feet moving rapidly at some distance, but I had so many things on my mind that I hardly gave a thought to the strangeness of such a noise at two o'clock in the morning.

Doctor Kenneth, a plain, rough man, was luckily just coming out of his house to see a sick man in the village. He turned back with me.

'Nelly Dean,' he said, 'I can't help thinking there is another cause for this. A healthy girl like Catherine doesn't become ill for nothing. What started it?'

'The master will tell you,' I replied carefully, 'but you know the Earnshaws' violent natures, and Mrs Linton is worse than any of them.'

On examining the case for himself, he spoke to Mr Linton of her return to health, if only we could keep her completely quiet. To me, he said the danger was not so much of death as of lasting damage to the mind.

I did not close my eyes that night, nor did Mr Linton: in fact, we never went to bed, and the servants were all up long before the usual hour. Everybody was active except Miss Isabella, and we all began to notice how deeply she slept. Her brother, too, asked if she had got up, and seemed hurt by her lack of anxiety for Catherine.

One of the servants, a thoughtless girl, came crying up the stairs: 'Oh! Oh! What will we have next? Master, master, our young lady—'

'Less noise!' I exclaimed quickly.

'Speak quietly, Mary. What's the matter?' said Mr Linton.

'She's gone! She's gone! Heathcliff's run off with her!' cried the girl.

The girl had been to the village, and had met the boy who brought the milk. He had told of how a gentleman and a lady had stopped to have a horseshoe fixed two miles out of Gimmerton not long after midnight. There was no mistaking Heathcliff, and the covering over the lady's head had fallen back when she took a drink, and shown her face clearly.

'Shall we try and fetch her back?' I asked. 'What should we do?'

'She went of her own free will,' answered the master. 'Trouble me no more about her. In future she is my sister in name only.'

He made no further mention of her to me, except to direct me to send what property she had in the house to her new home, wherever it was, when I knew it.

Chapter 16   Two Bad Months

For two months the runaway pair remained absent, and during those two months Mrs Linton suffered and gradually recovered from the worst shock of what was found to be a brain fever. Day and night Edgar watched over her, patiently bearing all the difficulties of temper caused by illness of both body and mind. The doctor warned him that his own health and strength were being destroyed for nothing, because his wife would never be the same again, but his joy knew no limits when Catherine's life was declared out of danger. There was double cause for joy, as another life depended on hers; and we hoped that in a little time Mr Linton's heart would be gladdened, and his lands made safe from the hands of a stranger, by the birth of a son.

The first time she left her room was at the beginning of March. Mr Linton had put a handful of flowers beside her bed in the morning. Her eye caught the bright colour on waking, and shone with pleasure.

'These are the earliest flowers at the Heights,' she exclaimed. 'They remind me of soft winds and warm sunshine and nearly melted snow.'

'The snow has quite gone, my dearest,' said her husband. 'Catherine, last spring I was looking forward eagerly to having you under this roof. Now I wish you were a mile or two up those hills. The air blows so sweetly, I feel it would cure you.'

The master told me to light a fire in the sitting room and place a chair in the sunshine. He brought her down, and she sat a for while, enjoying the heat. By evening, although very tired, she refused to return upstairs, so another room was prepared for her on the same floor. She was soon strong enough to move from one to the other, leaning on Edgar's arm.

About six weeks after Isabella had left, she sent her brother a note, announcing her marriage to Heathcliff. It appeared dry and cold, but at the bottom was a line in pencil, expressing her sorrow for what she had done and a desire for forgiveness. Linton did not reply, and two weeks later I got a letter from the unhappy girl, which I have kept until now.

'Dear Ellen,' it began, 'I came last night to Wuthering Heights and heard for the first time that Catherine has been, and is still, very ill. I must not write to her, I suppose, and my brother is either too angry or too unhappy to answer what I send him.

'Inform Edgar that my heart returned to the Grange twenty-four hours after I left. I can't follow it, though.

'I do not know how you managed, when you lived here, to remain human. Is Heathcliff mad or is he a devil? I beg you to explain, if you can, what I have married.

'We got here after sunset. Joseph brought out a light, gave me an ugly look, and took away the horses. Heathcliff stayed to speak to him, and I entered the kitchen, a dirty, untidy hole. I dare say you wouldn't recognize it: it is so changed since it was in your care. By the fire stood a rough-looking, dirty child, rather like Catherine in the eyes and around the mouth, whom I realized must be Hareton. I tried to make friends, but he first cursed and then set a dog on me.

'I wandered round the yard, and knocked at a door. It was opened by a tall man, very untidily dressed, with long uncut hair. He, too, was like our Catherine. It was her brother. He let me in and shut the door. I saw I was in the large room that used to look so bright and cheerful when I visited it years ago. Now it is dusty and uncared for. I asked if I could call a servant and be shown to a bedroom. Mr Earnshaw did not answer. He appeared to have forgotten my presence, and seemed so strange and unwelcoming that I did not want to interrupt him again.

'I remembered that four miles away lay my lovely home, containing the only people I love on earth; but there might as well be the ocean between us!

'Finally I repeated my question.

'"We have no female servants," said Earnshaw. "You must look after yourself."

'"Where must I sleep, then?" I wept. I was tired and miserable.

'"Joseph will show you Heathcliff's room" he replied. "I would be grateful if you would turn your key and lock the door."

'"But why, Mr Earnshaw?" I asked.

'"Look here!" he said, pulling a small gun from his pocket. "I can't help going up with this every night and trying his door. If once I find it open, he'll be a dead man!"

'"What has Heathcliff done to you?" I asked. "Wouldn't it be wiser to order him to leave the house?"

'"No!" shouted Earnshaw. "Am I to lose all my money, without a chance of winning it back? Is Hareton to have nothing? I will have it back, and I'll have his gold, too, and his blood!"

'You know your old master's habits, Ellen. He is clearly close to madness. I'm afraid to be near him.

'Heathcliff's room was locked. I went to sleep in a chair in the sitting room until he came in with the news of Catherine's illness and accused my brother of causing it. He promised to punish me instead of him, until he could get hold of him.

'I am miserable – I have been foolish! Say nothing of this to anyone at the Grange. Call and see me, Ellen, very soon. I shall expect you every day – don't disappoint me!

ISABELLA.'

Chapter 17   A Visit to Wuthering Heights

As soon as I had finished Isabella's letter, I went to the master and gave him the news of his sister and her wish for some sign of his forgiveness.

'I have nothing to say to her, Ellen,' was his reply. 'You may call this afternoon and say I'm sorry I've lost her. We are now divided for ever.'

Mr Edgar's coldness saddened me very greatly, and all the way to Wuthering Heights I worried my brains as to how to soften his answer.

There was never such a miserable scene as the house, formerly so cheerful, presented on my arrival. The young lady already shared the appearance of disorder that surrounded her. Her pretty face was pale and expressionless, her hair uncurled, some hanging down and some carelessly twisted round her head. Probably she had not tidied her dress since the evening before.

Hindley was not there, but Mr Heathcliff sat at a table. He rose and offered me a chair. He was the only thing that seemed respectable, and I thought he had never looked better. A stranger would have thought him a born gentleman and his wife a person of low origin.

She came forward, half expecting a letter, and I had to tell her her brother's words. Her lip trembled and she returned to her seat.

Her husband began questioning me about Catherine.

'Mrs Linton is now just recovering,' I told him. 'She'll never be like she was, but her life is saved. Her appearance is greatly changed, her character more so, and the person who is forced to be her companion will only keep up his love for her by remembering what she was formerly, and by pity and a sense of duty.'

Heathcliff forced himself to appear calm.

'Do you imagine I shall leave Catherine to your master's duty and pity! Nelly, I must have a promise from you that you'll arrange for me to see her. Agree or refuse, I *will* see her! What do you say?'

'I say, Mr Heathcliff,' I replied, 'that another meeting and quarrel between you and Mr Linton would kill her altogether.'

'With your help that may be avoided,' he said. 'The fear that she would suffer from his loss keeps me from doing my worst. And there you see the difference between our feelings. If he had been in my place, and I in his, I would never have raised a hand against him as long as she desired his company. The moment her feeling had ended, I would have torn his heart out, but until then – I would have died before I touched a single hair of his head!'

'Even so,' I interrupted, 'you don't care about ruining her chances of returning to health, by seeing her when she has nearly forgotten you.'

'Oh, Nelly! You know she has not! You know as well as I do that for every thought she spends on Linton, she spends a thousand on me! I feared last summer that she might have forgotten me, but now only her own words would make me believe such a horrible idea. And then – Linton would be nothing, or Hindley, or all the other dreams of revenge that I ever dreamed. One word would represent my future – *death*. But Catherine has a heart as deep as I have. Linton is hardly a degree nearer to her than her dog, or her horse. It is not in him to be loved like me: how then can she love in him what he has not?'

'Catherine and Edgar are as fond of each other as any two people can be!' cried Isabella, with a sudden return to life. 'I won't hear my brother spoken of so lightly!'

'Your brother is very fond of you, isn't he?' said Heathcliff scornfully.

'My young lady is looking sadly the worse for her change of condition,' I said. 'I hope you will consider that she is used to being looked after. You must let her have a servant. Whatever you think of Mr Edgar, you cannot doubt her powers of love, or she would never have given up the comforts of her home to live in this wild place with you.'

'She gave them up under a false idea of me as the sort of man she has read about in stories,' he answered. 'I can hardly look on her as being sensible, so fixed is the idea she has formed of my character. But at last I think she is beginning to know me. I don't care who knows that the feeling was all on one side, and I never lied to her about it. The first thing she saw me do, on coming out of the Grange, was to hang up her little dog, but even that didn't make her hate me. Tell your master, Nelly, that I never in all my life met such a poor-spirited thing as she is. She brings shame even on the name of Linton!'

'He says he married me on purpose to gain power over Edgar,' cried Isabella. 'But he shan't do so! I just hope he'll kill me! The only pleasure I can imagine is to die, or to see him dead!'

'If you're called on in a court of law, you'll remember her language, Nelly!' said Heathcliff coldly. 'And take a good look at her face: she's near the point that would suit me. You're not responsible for your actions now, Isabella, and I, as your lawful husband, must keep you safe. Go upstairs. I have something to say to Ellen in private.'

He pushed her from the room.

'I have no pity,' he murmured. 'I have no pity! The more the worms suffer, the more I desire to crush them.'

I rose to go.

'Stop!' he said. 'Come here, Nelly. I must either persuade or force you to help me to see Catherine. I don't wish to cause any quarrels. I'd warn you when I came, and then you might let me in unnoticed, as soon as she was alone.'

I argued and complained, and firmly refused him fifty times, but in the end Heathcliff forced me to an agreement. I was to carry a letter from him to my mistress, and, if she agreed, to send him news of Linton's next absence from home, when he could come and see her.

Chapter 18   The Meeting

That evening I knew, as well as if I saw him, that Mr Heathcliff was around the Grange, and I avoided going outside because I was still carrying his letter in my pocket. Until my master went somewhere, I did not want to give it, because I could not guess how it would affect my mistress. It did not reach her, therefore, until three days had passed.

The fourth was Sunday, and I brought it into her room after the household had gone to church.

Catherine sat in a loose white dress, at the open window as usual. Her long hair, cut shorter during her illness, was simply combed over her forehead and neck. Her appearance was changed, but when she was calm there seemed a strange beauty in the change. The flash in her eyes had given place to a dreamy softness. The paleness of her face, and the strange expression resulting from her state of mind, added to the interest she awakened, but to me they were unmistakable signs that her future was an early death.

Gimmerton church bells were still ringing, and the full flow of the little stream in the valley came sweetly to the ear. Catherine seemed to be listening, but she had the dreamy, distant look that I have mentioned.

'There's a letter for you, Mrs Linton,' I said, gently placing it in her hand. 'You must read it now, because it needs an answer. Shall I open it?'

'Yes,' she answered, without changing the direction of her eyes.

I did so, and gave it to her. She pulled away her hand and let it fall.

I replaced it on her knee, and stood waiting.

At last I said, 'Must I read it? It is from Mr Heathcliff.'

There was a sudden movement, and a troubled flash of memory, and a struggle to arrange her ideas. She lifted the letter and seemed to read it, and when she came to the name at the end she drew in her breath: but still I found she had not understood its meaning. She pointed to the name, and fixed her eyes on me with sad and questioning eagerness.

'He wishes to see you,' I said. 'He's probably in the garden by this time and impatient to know your answer.'

As I spoke, I noticed a large dog, lying on the sunny grass below, raise its ears and then, smoothing them back, show by a movement of the tail that someone was coming whom it did not consider a stranger. Mrs Linton bent forward and listened breathlessly.

A step was heard in the hall. With indescribable eagerness Catherine directed her eyes towards the entrance to her room. In a moment Heathcliff was at her side and had her in his arms.

He neither spoke nor loosed his hold for several minutes. I saw he could hardly bear, for pure misery, to look into her face! He felt, from the moment he saw her, that there was no hope that she would recover. Her future was decided; she was sure to die.

'Oh, Cathy! Oh, my life! How can I bear it?' was the first sentence he spoke. And now he looked at her so deeply that I thought it would bring tears to his eyes; but they burned with pain, they did not melt.

'What now?' said Catherine, leaning back, and returning his look with one of sudden anger. 'You and Edgar have broken my heart, Heathcliff! And now you both come to cry pity on me, as if you were the people in need of sympathy! I shall not pity you, not I. You have killed me – and are all the stronger for it, I think.

How many years do you mean to live after I am gone?'

Heathcliff had knelt on one knee. He attempted to rise, but she seized his hair and kept him down.

'I wish I could hold you,' she continued bitterly, 'until we were both dead! I wouldn't care what you suffered. Why shouldn't you suffer? I do! Will you forget me? Will you be happy when I am in the earth?'

'Don't make me as mad as yourself!' he cried, forcing his head free. 'Are you possessed by a devil, to talk like that when you are dying? Do you realize that all those words will be burned into my memory? You know it is not true that I have killed you: and Catherine, you know that I could as easily forget you as my own existence! Is it not enough for your cursed selfishness that while you are at peace I shall be in misery?'

'I shall not be at peace,' murmured Catherine, brought back to a sense of weakness by the violent uneven beating of her heart. She said no more until the attack was over, then she continued, more kindly: 'I'm not wishing you greater pain than I have, Heathcliff. I only wish us never to be parted: and if the memory of any word of mine should give you pain in the future, think that I feel the same pain beneath the earth, and forgive me! Come here and kneel down again! You have never harmed me in your life.'

Heathcliff went to the back of her chair and leaned over, but not so far as to let her see his face, which was deathly white. She bent round to look at him; he would not allow it. Turning quickly he walked to the fireplace, where he stood silent with his back towards us. Catherine looked at him, then after a pause she spoke to me in an offended voice.

'You see, Nelly, he will not give way for a moment. That is how I'm loved. Well, never mind. That is not my Heathcliff. I shall love mine still. I am surprised he won't be near me,' she went on to herself. 'I thought he wished it. Heathcliff, dear, do come to me.'

In her eagerness she rose and supported herself on the arm of the chair. At that request he turned to her, looking completely miserable. For a moment they stayed apart, then how they met I hardly saw. Catherine seemed to jump, and he caught her and held her as if he would never let her go again. I thought my mistress had fainted, but when I approached to see he turned on me and pulled her closer to him, half mad with jealousy, so I stood to one side, not knowing what to do.

Soon a movement of Catherine's made me feel a little happier. She put her hand to his neck to bring his cheek to hers, while he said wildly: 'You teach me how cruel you've been – cruel and false! Why did you scorn me? Why were you false to your own heart, Cathy? I have not one word of comfort. You deserve this! You have killed yourself. Yes, you may kiss me, and cry, and force me to do the same – it is your punishment. You loved me – then what *right* had you to leave me? Because misery, and degradation, and death could not have parted us, *you* did it! I have not broken your heart – you have broken it, and in breaking it, you have broken mine. It is only the worse for me that I am strong. Do I want to live? Would *you* want to live with your soul in the grave?'

'Leave me alone,' wept Catherine. 'If I've done wrong, I'm dying for it. You left me too, but I forgive you. Forgive me!'

'It is hard, but I forgive you what you have done to me. I love my murderer – but yours! How can I?'

They were silent, their faces hidden against each other and washed by each other's tears. I became very uncomfortable, as the afternoon was passing and I could see in the sunshine up the valley a crowd of people outside the church.

'The service is over,' I said. 'Master will be here in half an hour.'

Heathcliff cursed and pulled Catherine closer. She never moved. Soon I saw a group of the servants coming up the road. Then

Edgar Linton opened the gate and walked through.

'Now he's here,' I exclaimed.

'I must go, Cathy,' said Heathcliff, 'but, as sure as I'm alive, I'll see you again before you are asleep. I shall be near your window.'

'You must not go!' she answered, holding him as firmly as her strength allowed.

'For one hour!' he begged.

'Not for one minute,' she replied.

'I must. Linton will be up immediately.'

He would have risen, but she hung fast. There was madness in her face. 'No! Oh, don't, don't go. It is the last time.'

Heathcliff murmured a curse on Edgar, and sank back into his seat.

'Quiet, my dearest! I'll stay. If he shot me now, I'd die happy.'

I heard my master coming up the stairs.

'She doesn't know what she says!' I cried. 'Will you ruin her, because she has not sense enough to help herself? Get up! We are all finished!'

Mr Linton heard the noise and came faster. I saw that Catherine's arms had fallen, and her head hung down.

'Either she's fainted or she's dead,' I thought.

Edgar jumped on his uninvited guest, white with shock and fury. What he meant to do, I cannot tell, but the other stopped him by placing the lifeless-looking form in his arms.

'Unless you are a devil,' he said, 'help her first – then speak to me.'

He walked into the sitting room. Edgar Linton called me, and with great difficulty we managed to bring Catherine back to life, though she recognized no one. Edgar, in his anxiety, forgot her hated friend. At the earliest opportunity I went to urge him to leave, saying that she was better and I would give him further news in the morning.

'I shall stay in the garden,' he answered. 'And, Nelly, if you do not keep your word, I shall pay another visit, whether Linton is in or not.'

Chapter 19   Heathcliff's Curse

At twelve o'clock that night a second Catherine, a weak, seven-month child, was born; and two hours after that the mother died, having never recovered enough consciousness to miss Heathcliff or to recognize Edgar. Her husband's grief was painful to see, and was greatly increased, in my opinion, by his being left without a son. In my mind I blamed old Mr Linton for fondly leaving his property, after Edgar's death, to his own daughter, and not to his son's daughter.

Soon after sunrise I went out wishing, though fearing, to find Heathcliff. He was leaning against a tree, his hair wet with the morning mist.

'She's dead,' he said. 'I've not waited for you to learn that. Put away your handkerchief. She wants none of your tears. How did–', he struggled with his grief, 'how did she die?'

'Poor unhappy soul,' I thought, 'you have a heart and feelings the same as other men!' I then replied aloud, 'Quietly as a lamb.'

'And – did she ever mention me?'

'Her senses never returned. She recognized no one from the time you left her. She lies with a sweet smile on her face, and her last spoken thoughts wandered back to pleasant days of her childhood.'

'May she wake in misery!' he cried, with terrible violence. 'She's a liar to the end! I pray one prayer – Catherine Earnshaw, may you not rest as long as I am living! You said that I killed you – be with me always, then! – take any form – drive me mad! Only do not leave me here, where I cannot find you! Oh God, I cannot live without my life!'

He struck his head against the tree trunk, not like a man but like a wild animal. The moment he recovered enough to notice me, he thundered a command for me to go, and I obeyed.

Catherine's funeral was planned for the Friday following her death. Until then, her coffin lay uncovered in the largest room downstairs. Edgar spent his days and nights there, a sleepless protector, while Heathcliff, as only I knew, watched, equally sleepless, outside.

On the Tuesday, a little after dark, when my master, extremely tired from watching, had gone to rest for an hour or two, I went and opened one of the windows to give Heathcliff a chance to say a last goodbye.

That he had silently done so I knew, when later I noticed on the floor a curl of fair hair, torn from the little heart-shaped gold case that hung on a chain round Catherine's neck. It was her husband's, and Heathcliff had thrown it out and replaced it by black hair of his own. I twisted the two, and enclosed them together.

Mr Earnshaw was invited to see the body of his sister to the grave, but he never came. Isabella was not asked.

Catherine was laid in the earth, to the surprise of the villagers, neither in the church with the Linton family, nor outside with her own relations. Her grave was dug on a green slope in a corner of the churchyard where the wall is so low that wild plants have climbed over it from the moor.

That Friday was the last of our fine days for a month. In the evening the weather changed. The wind brought first rain and then snow. It seemed that winter had returned.

The next day my master remained in his room. I was in the lonely sitting room, with the crying baby, when suddenly the door opened and someone entered, breathless and laughing. It was Isabella Heathcliff.

She came forward to the fire, holding her hand to her side.

'I've run the whole way from Wuthering Heights,' she said. 'Don't worry! I'll explain in a moment, only just be so kind as to step out and order transport to take me on to Gimmerton, and tell a servant to find a few of my clothes.'

Her hair streamed on her shoulders, wet with snow and water. She was dressed in the girlish silk dress she usually wore, more suited to her age than her position. It was very wet. She had a deep cut under one ear, and her face had the marks of a blow.

When I had treated her wound and helped her to change her clothes, and she was seated by the fire with a cup of tea, she began to talk, but first she begged me to take poor Catherine's baby into another room.

'I don't like to see it!' she said. 'You mustn't think I care little for Catherine, because I behaved so foolishly on entering. I've cried too, bitterly. But I wasn't going to sympathize with Heathcliff. This is the last thing of his that I have with me.'

She slipped the gold ring from her third finger and threw it into the fire with childish hate.

'Necessity forced me to come here for shelter, but I daren't stay,' she went on. 'Heathcliff is quite likely to follow in search of me, to annoy Edgar. And besides, Edgar has not been kind, has he? I won't come begging for help, and I won't bring him more trouble. Heathcliff hates the sight of me, and I feel fairly certain that he wouldn't chase me across England, if I managed a clear escape, so I must get far away from here.'

I inquired what had urged her to come away from Wuthering Heights in such a condition.

'I was forced to do so,' she replied. 'I had succeeded in exciting his fury beyond his ability to control himself. Since last Sunday he has not eaten a meal with us. He has been out every night, has come home in the early morning and locked himself in his room. Though I was full of grief for Catherine, it was impossible to avoid thinking of the week as a holiday. I was able to move freely about the house and to sit in peace by the fire.

'Last night I stayed up late reading. Hindley, who was less drunk than usual, sat opposite, his head in his hands. He is quieter now than formerly, if nobody annoys him. The silence was broken at last by the sound of Heathcliff at the kitchen door. I suppose he had returned earlier on account of the weather.

'The door was locked. My companion turned and looked at me.

'"I'll keep him out for five minutes," he exclaimed. "You and I each have a great debt to settle with the man outside. Are you as soft as your brother? Are you prepared to suffer to the end, without revenge?"

'"I'm tired of suffering," I answered, "and I'd be glad of a revenge that would not bring harm to myself; but violence wounds those who use it."

'"I'll ask you to do nothing," he replied, "but sit still and be silent. Promise to hold your tongue, and before that clock strikes – it is three minutes to one – you're a free woman!"

'He pulled from inside his coat the little gun which he had shown me on the night of our arrival. He then began to blow out the candles. I pulled his arm.

'"I'll not hold my tongue," I said. "You mustn't touch him. Be quiet!"

'"I've made up my mind," he cried. "It's time to make an end."

'It was useless for me to struggle with him. I could only run and open the window.

'"You'd better find shelter somewhere else," I called out, rather joyfully. "Mr Earnshaw is planning to shoot you."

'Heathcliff, with a curse, ordered me to let him in. I shut the window and returned to my place by the fire. Hindley swore at me, saying that I still loved the devil.

'A blow from Heathcliff broke the window and his dark face looked furiously through. The bars were too close together for his body to follow, and I smiled, imagining myself safe.

'"Isabella, let me in," he commanded.

'"I can't be responsible for murder," I answered. "Hindley stands waiting with a loaded gun. And that's a poor love of yours that cannot bear a little snow. Heathcliff, if I were you, I'd go and stretch myself over her grave and die like a loyal dog!"

'I could not move with terror at the results of my insulting words, when Heathcliff leaned in and seized Hindley's weapon from him. The gun exploded. Heathcliff took a stone and broke down the wooden frame between two windows, and jumped in.'

Chapter 20   Isabella Escapes

'Hindley had fallen unconscious with pain. Blood flowed from a large wound in his arm. Heathcliff kicked him, holding me with one hand to prevent me from fetching Joseph. At last, he dragged the seemingly lifeless body on to a chair, and put a cloth round the wound with cruel roughness. Freed for the moment, I went in search of the old servant.

'"Your master's mad," shouted Heathcliff, "and if he lives for another month, I'll have him put in a madhouse. Wash that away." He gave Joseph a push on to his knees in the middle of the blood, and turned to me.

'"You shall help, too," he said. "You join with him against me, do you?"

'He shook me violently.

'Later, Hindley showed signs of life, and Heathcliff, knowing that he could not remember the treatment received while he was unconscious, blamed him for being drunk, and advised him to get to bed.

'This morning, when I came down, Hindley was sitting by the fire, deathly sick. His enemy, looking almost as ill, leaned against the chimney. Heathcliff did not look at me. His eyes were dull with sleeplessness and weeping, and his lips closed in an expression of indescribable sadness. If it had been anyone else, I would have covered my face in the presence of such grief. In his case, I felt pleasure. I couldn't miss this chance of causing him pain.

'Hindley wanted some water. I handed him a glass, and asked him how he was feeling.

'"Not as ill as I wish," he replied. "But besides my arm, every bit of my body is sore."

'"Your enemy kicked you last night, and threw you on the floor," I told him. "It's enough that he has murdered one of you," I went on aloud. "At the Grange, everyone knows that your sister would have been living now, if it had not been for Mr Heathcliff."

'Heathcliff's attention was awakened. He wept, and I laughed.

'"Get out of my sight!" he said.

'"If poor Catherine had trusted you, and accepted the degrading title of Mrs Heathcliff," I continued, "she would soon have sunk into a state similar to her brother's. She wouldn't have borne your shameful behaviour quietly!"

'Heathcliff made a sudden movement. He picked up a dinner knife from the table and threw it at my head. It struck me beneath my ear and stopped the words I was about to say. I ran to the door. The last sight I had of him was a furious rush by him, prevented by Hindley. They both fell together. I ran through the kitchen, knocking over Hareton, and escaped down the steep road, then straight across the moor, rolling over banks, struggling through pools of water, aiming for the shelter of the Grange. And I would rather it were my fate to live for ever in misery than, even for one night, remain beneath the roof of Wuthering Heights again.'

Isabella ended her story and took a drink of tea. Then she rose and, taking no notice of my wish that she should remain for another hour, stepped on to a chair, kissed the pictures of Edgar and Catherine hanging on the wall, did the same to me, and went downstairs.

She was driven away, never to revisit the area, but when things were more settled there was a regular exchange of letters between her and my master. I believe she lived in the south, near London. There she had a son born a few months later. It was named Linton, and from the first it was a weak, complaining little thing.

Heathcliff, meeting me one day in the village, inquired where she lived. I refused to tell him, but he discovered, through some of the other servants, both where she was and of the existence of the child. Still he left her alone, though he often asked how the baby was.

'I'll have it when I want it,' he said.

Fortunately, the mother died before that time came.

◆

Grief, and a dislike of going anywhere that he was likely to meet Heathcliff, caused my master to lead a lonely life. He avoided the village, remaining within the limits of his own grounds, except for walks by himself on the moors and visits to the grave of his dead wife. Time gradually closed the wound, with the help of his daughter, who soon became queen of his heart. She was named Catherine, but he always called her Cathy, to make her name different from her mother's.

The end of Hindley was what might have been expected. It followed six months after his sister's. I found it hard to realize that he was only twenty-seven at the time.

When I requested permission to go to Wuthering Heights and help in the last duties to the dead, Mr Linton did not want to agree, but I spoke of Hindley's friendless condition, and said that my old master had a claim on my services as strong as his own. Besides, I reminded him, the child Hareton was his wife's nephew, and he ought to take care of him. He must inquire how the property was left, and find out the state of his brother-in-law's affairs. He told me to speak to Mr Green, his lawyer, and finally allowed me to go.

His lawyer had been Hindley's too. I called at the village, and asked him to go with me. He shook his head and advised that Heathcliff should be left alone, saying that, if the truth were known, Hareton would receive nothing from Hindley.

'His father died in debt,' he said. 'The whole property is held by someone else, and the only chance for the son is to allow him an opportunity of persuading that person to deal generously with him.'

When I reached the Heights, Joseph appeared glad to see me. Heathcliff said he did not consider my presence necessary, but as I had come I could stay and arrange for the funeral if I wished.

'The fool locked the doors of the house against me yesterday, and spent the night drinking himself to death,' he said. 'Joseph and I broke in this morning. He was both dead and cold, so it was useless to go to further trouble about him.'

I insisted on the funeral being respectable. Heathcliff let me have my own way, but warned me to remember that the money for the whole affair came out of his pocket. His behaviour all through this was hard and cold, showing neither joy nor sorrow. It expressed, if anything, a stony satisfaction at a difficult piece of work well done. I noticed once, in fact, something like pride in his face.

It was when he was about to follow the coffin from the house. He lifted the unfortunate Hareton on to the table and murmured with strange pleasure, 'Now, my pretty boy, you are mine! We'll see if one tree won't grow as twisted as another, if it is blown by the same wind!'

The poor little thing was pleased, and touched his cheek fondly, but I guessed the meaning of his words and remarked, 'The boy must go back with me to Thrushcross Grange, sir.'

'Does Linton say so?' he demanded.

'Of course – he has ordered me to take him.'

'Well, you may tell your master that I have a wish to try my skill at bringing up a young one, so if he attempts to remove this one, my own must take its place.'

This threat to Isabella's child was enough to tie our hands. Edgar Linton, little interested at the beginning, spoke no more of taking Hareton.

The guest was now master of Wuthering Heights. He held firm possession, and proved to the lawyer that Hindley had given into his keeping every yard of land he possessed, for money to supply his mad fondness for card playing.

In that manner Hareton, who should now be the most important gentleman in the area, was reduced to a state of complete dependence on his father's enemy, and lives in his own house as a servant without wages, unable to do anything to help himself because of his friendlessness and his ignorance that he has been wronged.

PART 3   THE SECOND CATHERINE (1784–1801)

Continued by Mrs Ellen Dean

Chapter 21   Cathy Rides Out

The twelve years that followed were the happiest of my life. My greatest troubles came from our little lady's small illnesses, which she had to experience like any other child. For the rest, after the first six months, she grew tall and straight, and could walk, and talk too in her own way, before the flowers came out for the second summer on her mother's grave. She was the loveliest thing that ever brought sunshine into an unhappy house: a real beauty, with the Earnshaws' dark eyes but the Lintons' fair skin and delicate face and yellow curling hair. Her spirits were high, but not rough, and her heart was kind and loving. It must be admitted that she had her faults, and she was as spoilt as any child that always got her way. I don't believe her father ever spoke a severe word to her. He took complete charge of her education. Curiosity and a quick intelligence made her a good pupil. She learned rapidly and did honour to his teaching.

Until she reached the age of thirteen, she had not once been beyond the park by herself. Her father would take her with him outside, on rare occasions, but he trusted her to no one else. She had never been to the village, and the church was the only building she had entered. Wuthering Heights and Mr Heathcliff did not exist for her.

Although she seemed happy enough with her sheltered life, she would sometimes stare out of her window upstairs and ask: 'How long will it be before I can walk to the top of those hills, Ellen? What are those rocks like when you stand under them?'

One of the servants told her about the wonderful underground hollow in the rocks. Our little lady begged her father to let her go, and he promised that she could go when she was older. But Miss Cathy measured her age by months, not years, and was continually repeating her request. The road to these rocks ran close to Wuthering Heights. Edgar could not bear to pass the place, so he continued to refuse.

The Linton family were by nature delicate. Isabella lived only twelve years after leaving her husband. When her last illness came on her, she wrote to her brother and begged him to come to her, if possible, as she wished to say goodbye to him and deliver her son safely into his hands. Her hope was that the boy could be left with him, and that the father would show no interest.

Although my master did not like to leave home for ordinary calls, he did not think twice now. He set out immediately, leaving

Cathy in my particular care, with repeated orders that she must not wander out of the park, even if I went with her.

He was away three weeks. For the first day or two, my little lady sat in a corner in the library, too sad to read or play, and too quiet to give trouble. This was followed by a time of restlessness and, as I was too busy to run up and down amusing her, I got into the habit of sending her on her travels round the grounds, sometimes on foot and sometimes on a horse. When she returned I would listen with patience to the story of her adventures, real and imaginary.

I did not fear her leaving the grounds, because the gates were usually locked, and I thought that even if they were not, she would not dare to go out alone. In this belief I was wrong.

Cathy came to me one morning, at eight o'clock, and said that she was that day an Arab traveller, going to cross the desert, and I must give her plenty of food for herself and her horse and her three dogs. She rode off with the basket, laughing when I told her to be back early.

The naughty thing never made her appearance at teatime. One traveller, the oldest dog, returned, but there was no sign of Cathy or her horse. I sent people out to search in all directions, and at last went myself. A workman was busy at a fence on the edge of the grounds. I asked if he had seen our young mistress.

'I saw her in the morning,' he replied. 'She made her horse jump over the fence just here, where it is lowest, and rode out of sight.'

Chapter 22   First Visit to the Heights

I realized at once that Miss Cathy must have started for the rocks. I pushed through a space which the man was repairing, and walked mile after mile until I was in view of the Heights, but I could see no sign of her. The rocks lie about a mile and a half beyond the Heights, and I began to fear that night would fall before I could reach them.

'I wonder whether she has slipped while climbing,' I thought, 'and been killed, or broken her bones?'

My anxiety was painful, and at first I was truly glad to recognize, in hurrying past the farmhouse, the fiercest of our dogs lying under a window with a bleeding ear. I opened the gate and knocked violently at the door. A woman I knew, who had been a servant at the Heights since the death of Mr Hindley, answered.

'Ah!' she said. 'You've come looking for your little mistress. Don't be frightened. She's here safe, but I'm glad you're not the master.'

'He's not home, then?' I asked.

'No, no,' she replied. 'He won't return for an hour or more. Step in and rest a bit.'

I entered, and found my wandering lamb seated by the fire, in a little chair that had been her mother's. Her hat was hung against the wall, and she seemed perfectly at home, laughing and talking in the happiest manner imaginable to Hareton — now a great strong youth of eighteen — who was looking at her with a good deal of curiosity and surprise.

'Well, miss,' I exclaimed, hiding my joy under an angry look. 'This is your last ride, until your father comes back. I'll not trust you outside the house again, you naughty, naughty girl! Put that hat on and come home now.'

'What have I done?' she wept, losing her high spirits at once. 'Papa won't be cross with me — he's never unpleasant like you, Ellen.'

'No,' said the servant, 'don't be hard on the pretty one, Mrs Dean. We made her stop. She wished to ride back, afraid that you would be anxious, but Hareton offered to go with her and I thought he should as it's a rough road.'

'How long do I have to wait?' I went on, taking no notice. 'It will be dark in ten minutes.'

I picked up her hat, and moved towards her to put it on her, but she, seeing quite well that the people in the house were on her side, began dancing round the room. When I gave chase, she ran like a mouse over and under and behind the furniture. Hareton and the woman laughed, and Cathy joined them, making fun of me until I cried in great annoyance: 'Well, Miss Cathy, if you knew whose house this is, you'd be glad to get out.'

'It's your father's, isn't it?' she said, turning to Hareton.

'No,' he replied, looking down as his face turned red.

'Whose then – your master's?' she asked.

His face became redder still, and he turned away.

'I thought he was the owner's son,' the naughty girl continued to me. 'He talked of "our" house, and he never said "miss" to me. He should have done, shouldn't he, if he's a servant?'

Hareton looked as black as a thundercloud.

'Now get my horse,' she said, 'and you may come with me. Hurry! What's the matter?'

With a curse, the youth told her he was not her servant.

Cathy could not believe what she had heard. She, who was always "queen" and "dearest" at home, to be insulted!

'But Ellen,' she cried, 'how dare he speak to me like that? You wicked thing, I shall tell my father what you said!'

Hareton did not seem to feel this threat, so tears came to her eyes.

'You bring my horse,' she exclaimed, turning to the woman.

'Take care, miss,' she answered. 'You'll lose nothing by being polite. Mr Hareton is your cousin, and I was never hired to serve you.'

'*He* my cousin!' cried Cathy, with a scornful laugh. 'My father has gone to fetch my cousin from London.'

I was much annoyed with her and the servant for what they

had made known to one another. I had no doubt that the expected arrival of Isabella's son would be reported to Mr Heathcliff, and I felt sure that on her father's return Cathy's first thought would be to ask an explanation of Hareton's claim to be a relation.

Hareton, recovering from his disgust at being mistaken for a servant, fetched her horse to the door and took, to please her, a fine little dog from the yard. Placing it in her arms, he told her that he did not mean any harm. She looked at him in disgust, and began to weep.

I could hardly help smiling that she should turn away from the poor fellow, who was an active youth, good-looking, strong and healthy, though dressed in clothes suited to his daily business of working on the farm. Still, I thought I could see in his face better qualities than his father ever possessed. Mr Heathcliff, I believed, had not done him any bodily harm, as a result of his fearless nature. He had directed all his energies to keeping the boy uneducated; he was never taught to read or write, never cured of any bad habit.

Miss Cathy refused the peace offering of the little dog, and we started for home. I could not find out from my little lady how she had spent her day except that, as I had thought, she had set out for the rocks, and that as she passed the farmhouse gate, Hareton had come out and his dogs had attacked hers. There was a fierce battle before their owners could separate them, and that formed an introduction. Cathy asked Hareton the way to the rocks, and he finally went with her.

I saw that Hareton had been a favourite until she had hurt his feelings. It took me a long time before I could persuade her not to mention the matter to her father. I explained how he objected to everybody at Wuthering Heights, and how sorry he would be to hear that she had been there, and how, if she told him I had disobeyed his orders, perhaps he would be so angry that I would have to leave. Cathy could not bear this last possibility, so she promised to be silent and she kept her word. After all, she was a sweet little girl.

Chapter 23   Heathcliff Claims His Own

A letter edged in black announced the day of my master's return. Isabella was dead, and he wrote to tell me to arrange a room for his young nephew. Cathy was wild with joy at the idea of welcoming her father back, and meeting her 'real' cousin.

The day came, and my little mistress was so impatient that she made me walk all through the park to meet them.

They came into view at last. Miss Cathy shouted and held out her arms. Her father got down, nearly as eager as herself. While they exchanged loving greetings, I took a look at Linton. He was asleep, wrapped up in furs as if it were winter. He was a pale, delicate, girlish-looking boy, who might have been mistaken for my master's younger brother, they were so alike; but he had a sickly unpleasant look that Edgar Linton never had.

The sleeper, being woken at the house, was lifted to the ground by his uncle.

'This is your cousin Cathy, Linton,' he said, putting their little hands together. 'She's fond of you already. Try to be cheerful, now. The travelling is at an end.'

The boy stepped back from Cathy's welcome and put his fingers to his eyes. All three entered the house and went upstairs to the library, where tea was laid ready. I took off Linton's outdoor clothes and placed him at the table, but he began to cry.

'I can't sit on a hard chair,' he complained.

'Go to a more comfortable one, then, and Ellen will bring you your tea there,' said his uncle patiently.

Cathy carried a little seat and her cup to his side. At first she was silent, but that could not go on for long. She was determined to make a pet of her cousin, and she began touching his curls fondly, and kissing his cheek, and offering him tea from her cup, like a baby. This pleased him. He dried his eyes and smiled faintly.

'He'll do very well, if we can keep him, Ellen,' said the master to me, after watching them for a minute. 'The company of a child of his own age will put new life into him.'

'Yes, if only we can keep him,' I thought to myself, but I felt there was slight hope of that. I had no idea how the weak child would live at Wuthering Heights, between his father and Hareton.

Our doubts were soon decided.

I had just taken the children upstairs, and seen Linton asleep, when a servant stepped out of the kitchen and informed me that Mr Heathcliff's man Joseph was at the door and wished to speak to the master.

Very slowly I went up to the library and announced the unwanted visitor. Joseph followed close on my heels and without invitation pushed past me, saying: 'Heathcliff sent me for his boy, and I mustn't go back without him.'

Edgar Linton was silent for a minute. An expression of great sorrow spread over his face. He felt bitter grief at the idea of giving up the boy, but could not see any way of keeping him.

'Tell Mr Heathcliff,' he answered calmly, 'that his son shall come tomorrow to Wuthering Heights. He is in bed, and too tired to go the distance now.'

With some difficulty Joseph was persuaded to go away empty-handed, but with the parting threat that Heathcliff himself would come over the next day to get his son.

To avoid the danger of this threat being carried out, Mr Linton ordered me to take the boy home early, on Cathy's horse. He added: 'You must say nothing to my daughter of where he has gone.

She cannot see him in future. Simply tell her that his father sent for him suddenly, and he has had to leave us.'

Young Linton was very unhappy about being woken from his sleep at five o'clock in the morning, and surprised to find he must prepare for further travelling. I softened the matter by saying that he was going to spend some time with his father, who wanted to see him without delay.

'My father!' cried the boy. 'I never knew that I had a father. Why didn't my mother and he live together, as other people do?'

'He had business to keep him in the north,' I answered, 'and your mother's health made it necessary for her to live in the south.'

The boy was not satisfied.

'She didn't speak to me about him,' he repeated. 'She often talked of Uncle, and I learned to love him. How can I love my father?'

'All children love their parents,' I said. 'Let's hurry. An early ride on a beautiful morning is better than another hour's sleep.'

'Is she going with us – the little girl I saw yesterday?'

'Not now.'

'Is Uncle?'

'No. I shall be your companion.'

Linton sank back on his pillow. 'I won't go without Uncle,' he said.

I had to call for my master's help in getting him out of bed. The poor thing was got off in the end with promises that his visit would be short, that his uncle and Cathy would visit him, and other promises, equally without truth, that I invented from time to time. At last, in the pure air and the sunshine, he began to brighten on the way and to put questions about his new home. Was Wuthering Heights as pleasant a place as Thrushcross Grange? Was his father as good-looking as his uncle?

'The house is not quite so large,' I told him, 'but it is the second in the neighbourhood. Your father is as young as your uncle, but he has black hair and eyes and looks more severe. He'll not seem so kind and gentle at first, perhaps, because it's not his nature, but of course he'll be fonder of you than any uncle, since you are his own.'

The boy was fully occupied with his own thoughts for the rest of the ride. It was half past six when we arrived. The household had just finished breakfast. The servant was taking away the things.

'Hullo, Nelly!' cried Mr Heathcliff when he saw me. 'You've brought my property, have you? Let me see it.'

He got up and came to the door. Hareton and Joseph followed, full of curiosity. Poor Linton took a quick, frightened look at all three.

'Surely,' said Joseph, after a careful examination, 'he's changed with you, master, and sent you his girl!'

Heathcliff gave a scornful laugh, and a curse.

'What a beauty! What a pretty little thing!' he exclaimed. 'It's worse than I expected!'

I told the trembling child to get down and enter. He did not quite understand his father's speech, and he was still not quite certain that this hard, scornful stranger was his father, but he held on to me with growing fear, and when Mr Heathcliff took a seat and ordered him to come to him, he hid his face in my shoulder and wept.

'Come!' said Heathcliff, stretching out a hand and dragging him roughly between his knees. 'None of that nonsense. We're not going to hurt you, Linton — isn't that your name? You're completely like your mother. Where is my share in you?'

He took off the boy's cap and pushed back his thick fair curls and felt his thin arms and small fingers. Linton stopped crying and lifted his great blue eyes to examine the examiner.

'Do you know me?' asked Heathcliff.

'No,' said Linton, with a look of fear.

'No? What a shame your mother never helped you to love me! You are my son. Be a good boy, and I'll look after you. Nelly, if you are tired, sit down. If not, get home. This thing won't be settled while you're still about.'

'Well,' I replied, 'I hope you'll be kind to the boy, Mr Heathcliff, or he won't live long.'

'I'll be *very* kind to him, you needn't fear,' he said, laughing. 'And to begin my kindness – Joseph! Bring the boy some breakfast. Hareton! Get to your work.'

'Yes,' he added when they had gone, 'my son is the future owner of your place, and I would not wish him to die until I am certain of receiving it from him. Besides, he's *mine*, and I want the pleasure of seeing my son fairly lord of *their* property, *my* child hiring their children to look after their fathers' lands for wages. It's only such a thought that makes me able to bear the miserable thing. He's worthless in himself, and I hate him for the memories he brings back! But he's safe with me. I have a room upstairs, finely decorated for him. I've hired a teacher to come three times a week. I've ordered Hareton to obey him. In fact, I've arranged everything to keep him a gentleman. It is a pity, though, that he so little deserves the trouble. If I wished for anything in the world, it was to find him a worthy object of pride, and I'm bitterly disappointed in the milk-faced baby!'

While he was speaking, Joseph returned with some food and placed it in front of Linton. Linton looked at the food with disgust and declared he could not eat it. Joseph was angry, but Heathcliff ordered the housekeeper to give him whatever he wanted to eat. Having no excuse for staying any longer, I slipped out while Linton was looking at a friendly sheepdog. But as I closed the door, I heard a cry and a repetition of the words: 'Don't leave me! I won't stay here! I won't stay here!'

Chapter 24　'Will You Walk into My House?'

We had sad work with little Cathy that day. She rose in a state of excitement, eager to join her cousin, and floods of tears followed the news that he had gone.

Whenever I chanced, from time to time, to meet the housekeeper from Wuthering Heights in the village, I used to ask how the young master was, as he lived almost as sheltered a life as Cathy herself and was never to be seen. I learned that he was in weak health and was a difficult person to look after. Mr Heathcliff seemed to dislike him more and more, though he took some trouble to hide it. He could not bear to be in the same room as him for long. Linton learned his lessons and spent his evenings in a small room of his own, or else lay in bed all day, as he was continually getting coughs and colds, and aches and pains of all sorts.

This housekeeper left two years after he came and another, whom I did not know, took her place.

Time passed at the Grange in its former pleasant way until Miss Cathy reached the age of sixteen. On her birthday we never had any kind of party, because it was also the day of her mother's death. Her father always spent it alone, and walked to the grave, so Cathy was left to amuse herself.

This was a beautiful spring day, and my young lady came down early, dressed for going out, saying that her father had given her permission to go on the edge of the moors with me, if we only went a short distance.

'So hurry, Ellen!' she said. 'There are some young birds up there. I want to see if they have made their nests yet.'

'That must be some distance away,' I answered. 'They don't nest on the edge of the moor.'

'No, it's not,' she said. 'I've gone very near with Papa.'

Thinking no more of the matter, I got myself ready and we set out. She ran backwards and forwards along the path, and at first I found plenty of entertainment in listening to the birds singing far and near, and enjoying the warm sunshine, and watching my little dear, with her golden curls flying loose behind, and her bright cheek, as soft and pure as a rose, and her eyes shining with pleasure. She was a happy being in those days.

'Well,' I said, 'where are your birds, Miss Cathy? We have come a long way.'

'Only a little farther — a little farther,' was her answer continually.

At last I began to grow tired, and called to her that we must go back. She did not listen, and I was forced to follow. She disappeared ahead of me into a hollow and when I next came in sight of her, she was two miles nearer Wuthering Heights than her own home. I saw two people stop her, one of whom was Mr Heathcliff.

Cathy had been caught stealing, or at least hunting for the birds on the Heights. This was Mr Heathcliff's land, and he was warning her. She showed him her empty hands.

'I've neither taken nor found any,' she said. 'My father told me there were plenty up here, and I wished to see the eggs.'

With an evil smile, Heathcliff asked who her father was.

'Mr Linton of Thrushcross Grange,' she replied. 'I thought you did not know me, or you wouldn't have spoken in that way.'

'You suppose that your father is highly respected?' he said scornfully.

'And who are you?' inquired Cathy. 'Is that man your son?'

She pointed at Hareton, who looked bigger and stronger than ever, but just as rough and awkward.

'Miss Cathy,' I interrupted, 'we must be getting back home now.'

'No, that man is not my son,' answered Heathcliff, paying no attention to me. 'But I have one, whom you have seen before. I think both you and your nurse will feel better after a little rest.

Will you walk into my house? You shall receive a kind welcome.'

I whispered to Miss Cathy that she must on no account accept this invitation, but she ran on, and Heathcliff had seized my arm.

'Mr Heathcliff, it's very wrong,' I said. 'You know you mean no good. And as soon as we return, I shall get the blame for this.'

'I want her to see Linton,' he replied. 'He's looking better these last few days. I want the two cousins to fall in love and get married. It's generous of me, as the girl will have nothing when her father dies.'

'Linton's life is quite uncertain,' I said, 'and if he died, Cathy would become the owner of the place.'

'No, she would not,' he returned. 'There is no arrangement in the will of that kind. The property would go to me, but to prevent arguments I desire them to marry.'

And he led me to the gate, where Miss Cathy was waiting for us.

Chapter 25   A Second Visit to the Heights

Cathy gave Mr Heathcliff some strange looks, as if she could not exactly decide what to think of him, but now he smiled and softened his voice when addressing her, and I was foolish enough to imagine that the memory of her mother might persuade him not to do her harm.

Linton stood by the fireplace. He had been walking in the fields, and was calling for Joseph to bring him dry shoes. He had grown tall, his face was still pretty, and his eyes and skin were healthier than I remembered.

'Now, who is that?' asked Mr Heathcliff, turning to Cathy.

Cathy looked doubtfully from one to the other.

'Your son?' she said.

'Yes,' he answered. 'You have a short memory. Linton, don't

you remember your cousin, whom you were always wishing to see?'

'What, Linton!' cried Cathy, in joyful surprise. 'Is that really little Linton? He's taller than I am!'

She ran forward and kissed him. They stared in wonder at the changes that time had made in their appearance. Cathy had reached her full height, and she shone with health. Linton's looks and movements lacked energy, but there was a certain attractiveness in his manner.

Cathy turned to Heathcliff. 'And you are my uncle, then!' she cried, reaching up to kiss him also. 'I thought I liked you, though you were unpleasant at first. Why don't you visit the Grange with Linton? Naughty Ellen!' she continued, turning to me. 'Wicked Ellen, to try to stop me from entering!'

'Don't waste your kisses on me,' said her uncle. 'I think I'd better tell you. Mr Linton has a low opinion of me. We quarrelled at one time in our lives. If you mention your visit here, he will forbid you to come again.'

'Why did you quarrel?' asked Cathy, surprised and disappointed.

'He thought me too poor to marry his sister,' answered Heathcliff, 'and was upset when I got her.'

'That's wrong!' said the young lady. 'Some time I'll tell him so. But Linton and I have no share in your quarrel. I'll not come here, but he shall come to the Grange.'

'It is too far,' said her cousin. 'To walk four miles would kill me.'

The father looked with bitter scorn at his son.

'Have you nothing to show your cousin?' he said. 'Take her into the garden before you change your shoes.'

'Wouldn't you rather sit here?' Linton asked Cathy.

'I don't know,' she replied, with a quick look at the door.

He kept his seat, and moved closer to the fire. Heathcliff rose and called out for Hareton. Hareton replied and soon appeared. He had been washing himself, as was noticeable by his shining cheeks and his wet hair.

'He's not my cousin, Uncle, is he?' cried Cathy.

'Yes,' he replied. 'Your mother's nephew. Don't you like him?'

Cathy looked uncertain. She reached up and whispered a sentence in Heathcliff's ear. He laughed, and Hareton's face became dark. But his master chased the displeasure away by exclaiming: 'You'll be the favourite among us, Hareton! She said something very nice about you. Go round the farm with her, and behave like a gentleman. Don't use any bad words, don't fix your eyes on her, speak slowly, and keep your hands out of your pockets.'

He watched the pair walking past the window. Hareton did not look at his companion. 'I've tied his tongue,' remarked Heathcliff with satisfaction. 'He'll be afraid to say a word. Nelly, you remember me at his age – no, a few years younger – did I ever look so stupid?'

'Worse,' I replied, 'because you were more evil-tempered.'

'I take pleasure in him,' he continued. 'If he were a born fool I would not enjoy it half as much. I can sympathize with all his feelings, having felt them myself. He'll never be able to escape from his roughness and ignorance, because I've taught him to take a pride in his condition. I control him more tightly than his father ever controlled me. And the best of it is, Hareton is extremely fond of me. If his father could rise from the grave and tell me I've wronged his child, that child would fight him to protect me as his one friend in the world!'

He gave a wicked laugh. Linton, perhaps unhappy about the loss of Cathy's company, began to be restless. He got up and went outside.

Cathy was asking Hareton what the words over the door were. Hareton looked up and stared at them.

'Some writing,' he answered. 'I can't read it.'

Linton gave a silly little laugh.

'He doesn't even know his letters,' he said to Cathy. 'Did you ever see anyone so ignorant? There's nothing the matter but laziness, is there, Hareton? Have you noticed his bad pronunciation? He scorns "book-learning", as he calls it.'

'Why? What's the use of it?' said Hareton.

Linton and Cathy burst into a noisy fit of laughter, and the poor, angry youth went away, his face burning with fury and shame. Mr Heathcliff smiled as he saw him go, but afterwards I saw him direct a look of hate at the heartless pair, who continued to enjoy their sense of superiority. I began to dislike, more than to pity Linton, and to excuse his father in some degree for thinking badly of him.

◆

We stayed until the afternoon. I could not get Miss Cathy away before. Luckily my master had remained in his room and knew nothing of our long absence.

Next day, though, the truth came out. I was not completely sorry. I thought the responsibility of directing and warning my young lady could be borne better by her father than by me, but he was too careful in giving reasons why she should avoid the people at the Heights, and Cathy liked good reasons for anything that prevented her having her own way. Finally Mr Linton told her of Heathcliff's treatment of Isabella. She appeared so surprised and upset at this new view of human nature that he thought it unnecessary to say any more about it.

She kissed her father and sat down quietly to her lessons for an hour or two; then she went with him for a walk in the grounds, and the whole day passed as usual. In the evening, though, when I went upstairs to help her undress, I found her crying on her knees by the bedside.

'Silly child!' I exclaimed. 'If you had any real griefs, you'd be ashamed to waste a tear on a little thing like this.'

'I'm not crying for myself, Ellen,' she answered. 'It's for Linton. He'll be so disappointed if he doesn't see me again.'

'Nonsense!' I said. 'He will guess what has happened and trouble himself no further about you.'

'But may I not write a few words to tell him why I can't come? And just send those books I promised to lend him?'

'No, you can't,' I replied decisively. 'Then he would write to you, and there would never be an end to it.'

'But how can one little letter—'

'Silence!' I interrupted. 'We'll not discuss your letters. Get into bed.'

She gave me a very naughty look, so naughty that at first I refused to kiss her goodnight. I covered her up and went away, shutting the door; but a little later, feeling sorry, I returned softly, and found Miss Cathy standing at the table with a piece of paper and a pencil in her hand, which she guiltily slipped out of sight when I came forward.

'You'll get nobody to take that, if you write it,' I said.

I put out her candle as I spoke, receiving as I did a little blow on my hand, and the name of 'cruel thing'.

Weeks passed, and Cathy recovered her temper, though she became very fond of creeping off into corners by herself and reading some book which she would bend over to hide if I came near, and which seemed to have sheets of paper pushed between the leaves. She also got into the habit of coming down early in the morning to the kitchen, as if she were expecting something, and she had a small drawer in a cupboard in the library which she would examine for hours, and whose key she took special care to remove when she left.

One day, as she examined this drawer, I noticed that the little playthings and other small possessions that had formerly been kept in it had mysteriously been changed into bits of folded paper. I wondered what she was keeping secret, and worried for her, so at night I found among my keys one that would fit the lock, and made an examination of her hiding place.

The drawer contained a pile of daily letters from Linton Heathcliff, answers to messages written by my young lady. I tied them up in a handkerchief and relocked the empty drawer.

Next morning I watched Miss Cathy go down to the kitchen and rush to the door on the arrival of a little boy who came to fetch milk. While the serving-girl filled his can, Miss Cathy put something in his pocket, and took something else out. I followed the boy out into the garden and succeeded in seizing the letter, though he fought bravely to defend his trust. I remained under the wall and read it. It was more simple and sincere than those of her cousin: very pretty and very silly.

The day was wet, so at the end of her morning studies Cathy went straight to her drawer to amuse herself. Her father sat reading at the table, and I, on purpose, was mending the border of a curtain by the window, keeping my eye fixed on all that happened.

Never did any bird flying back to a nest robbed of its young ones express more complete misery in all its cries than she by her single 'Oh!'

Mr Linton looked up.

'What is the matter, my dear?' he said. 'Have you hurt yourself?'

'No, Father,' she replied with difficulty. 'Ellen! Ellen! Come upstairs – I'm sick!'

I obeyed her call.

'Oh, Ellen, you have got them,' she began at once. 'Oh, give them to me, and don't tell my father! I've been extremely naughty, but I won't do it any more!'

'I'm going with them to the library,' I replied, 'and we'll see what your father says about this nonsense.'

She tried to take them from me, but I held them above my head. She begged that I would burn them – do anything rather than show them. At last, since I was as ready to laugh as to be cross, I said: 'Will you promise me not to send or receive a letter again, or a book, or curls of hair, or rings, or playthings?'

'We don't send playthings,' cried Cathy, her pride defeating her shame.

'Not anything at all, then, my lady!' I said.

'I promise, Ellen!' she cried, catching hold of my dress.

But when I began to put them on the fire, their destruction was too painful.

'Can't I keep one or two Ellen?'

I continued to drop them on the flames.

'I *will* have one, you cruel thing!' she exclaimed, putting her hand into the fire, and drawing out some half-burnt pieces, with some damage to her fingers.

'Very well – then I'll have some to show your father!'

At that, she emptied her blackened pieces into the flames and without speaking went away to her own room. I went down to tell my master that the young lady's attack of sickness was almost gone, but I judged it best for her to lie down for a time. At tea she appeared, pale and red about the eyes, and unusually quiet.

Next morning, I replied to Linton's letter with a short note: 'Master Heathcliff is requested to send no more letters to Miss Linton, as she will not receive them.'

And from that time, the little boy came and went with empty pockets.

Chapter 26   The Result of Climbing a Wall

Summer came to an end. The crops were brought in late that year. Mr Linton and his daughter frequently walked among the workers in the fields, and on the last day they stayed until night fell. As a result of this my master caught a bad cold, which settled on his lungs, keeping him indoors all through the winter.

Poor Cathy, frightened from her little love affair, had been sadder and duller since it had ended, and her father encouraged her to read less and take more exercise. She no longer had his companionship, and though I tried to make up for this, I had only two or three hours free from my many daily duties.

One afternoon at the beginning of November, when it looked likely to rain, I asked my young lady to give up her walk. She refused, so I put on my outdoor clothes to go with her to the bottom of the park. This was a walk she chose when she was feeling low-spirited, as now, when my master was worse than usual.

As we neared a door which opened on to the road, my lady became more cheerful, and climbed up and seated herself on top of the wall to pick some berries. She reached up to get them, and her hat fell off on the outer side. Since the door was locked, she suggested dropping down to get it. I told her to be careful of falling, and she disappeared.

But the return was not so easy. The stones of the wall outside were smooth and well joined. I didn't remember this until I heard her laughing and calling out: 'Ellen, you'll have to fetch the key, or else I must run round to the main gate.'

'Stay where you are,' I answered. 'I have my bunch of keys in my pocket. Perhaps I can manage to open it.'

I had tried all the keys without success when I heard the sound of a horse and Cathy whispered anxiously through the door: 'Ellen, I wish you could open it.'

'Hullo, Miss Linton!' cried a deep voice. 'I'm glad to meet you. I have an explanation to ask of you.'

'I shan't speak to you, Mr Heathcliff,' answered Cathy. 'Father says you are a wicked man, and you hate him and me; Ellen says the same.'

'That is not the point,' said Heathcliff. 'I don't hate my son, I suppose, and it is concerning him that I demand your attention. Yes! You have cause to go red! Two or three months ago, you were in the habit of writing to Linton. I've got your letters, and if you will not listen to me, I'll show them to your father. I suppose you grew tired of the amusement? Well, Linton was serious. He's dying for you – breaking his heart at your cruelty. He gets worse every day, and unless you do something to help him, he'll be under the ground before next summer.'

'How can you lie so shamelessly to the poor child!' I called out. 'Miss Cathy, I'll break this lock open with a stone in a minute. Don't believe his nonsense.'

'I didn't know that there was anyone listening,' murmured Heathcliff. 'Mrs Dean, how can you lie so shamelessly! Miss Linton, I shall be away from home all this week. Go and see if I have not spoken the truth.'

The lock broke, and I came out.

'Come in,' I said, taking Cathy by the arm, and half forcing her to enter, as she was looking with troubled eyes at the speaker.

I closed the door and, since the rain had begun, we hurried home in silence.

That evening, as we sat by the fire, she wept to herself. I argued with her without success. Heathcliff had done his work too skilfully.

'You may be right, Ellen,' she said, 'but I shall never feel at peace until I know.'

What use were anger and argument? Next day saw me on the road to Wuthering Heights, by the side of my young mistress's horse. I couldn't bear her sorrow, her pale face and heavy eye. I gave in, in the faint hope that Linton might prove, by his way of receiving her, how little truth there was in his father's words.

Chapter 27   Linton Is Difficult

The rainy night was followed by a misty morning, and the rushing streams from the hills crossed our path. My feet were thoroughly wet, and I felt uncomfortable and unwell. We entered the farmhouse by the kitchen door, to be sure that Heathcliff was really absent.

Joseph was sitting alone, in front of a huge fire, with his pipe in his mouth. He answered our questions with his usual bad temper.

'Joseph!' cried a complaining voice from the inner room. 'How often do I have to call you? The fire is going out.'

Joseph took no notice. The housekeeper and Hareton were not around, both probably at their work elsewhere. We recognized Linton's voice and entered.

His cousin flew to his side.

'Is that you, Miss Linton?' he said, raising his head from the arm of the great chair in which he was lying. 'Will you shut the door, please? You left it open, and those hateful people won't bring coal for the fire. It's so cold!'

I attended to the fire, and fetched some coal myself. The sick boy complained of being covered in ashes, but he had a bad cough and looked feverish and ill, so I did not blame him.

'Well, Linton,' said Cathy, 'are you glad to see me?'

'Why didn't you come before?' was his reply. 'You should have come, instead of writing. It tired me so much, writing those long letters. Now I can neither bear to talk, nor anything else. I wonder where Zillah is! Will you' – looking at me – 'step into the kitchen and see?'

I had received no thanks for my other service, so I remained where I was, replying, 'There is no one there except Joseph.'

'I want to drink,' he exclaimed, turning away. 'Zillah is always going off to Gimmerton since my father left. And I'm forced to come down here – they pretend not to hear me upstairs.'

Cathy began searching for some water. She filled a glass and brought it. He told her to add a spoonful of wine from a bottle on the table and, having swallowed a little, seemed better and said she was very kind.

'Are you glad to see me?' repeated Cathy, pleased that he was smiling faintly.

'Yes, I am,' he replied. 'But I have been annoyed that you haven't come before. And Father swore it was my fault. He called me a worthless thing, and said if he had been in my place, he would be more master of the Grange than your father by this time.'

'I dare not come while your father is here,' said Cathy. 'If I could get my father's permission, I'd spend half my time with you. I wish you were my brother!'

'And then you would like me as well as your father?' he remarked, more cheerfully. 'But Father says you would love me better than anyone else, if you were my wife.'

'People hate their wives sometimes,' said Cathy, 'but not their brothers and sisters.'

Linton declared that people never hated their wives, but Cathy repeated that they did, and gave as an example his own father's dislike of her aunt. I tried to stop her thoughtless tongue, but everything she knew came out.

Linton declared that her story was false.

'Father told me, and he does not tell untruths,' she answered angrily.

'My father scorns yours!' cried Linton.

'And yours is a wicked man!' replied Cathy.

'Well, I'll tell you something,' said Linton. 'Your mother hated your father: now then!'

'Oh!' exclaimed Cathy, too furious to continue.

'And she loved mine!' he added.

'It's not true!' she shouted. 'I hate you now.'

'She did! She did!' sang Linton, sinking back to enjoy the unhappiness of his companion, who stood behind him.

Cathy, losing control of herself, gave the chair a violent push and caused him to fall against one arm. At once he was seized with a cough that stopped his breath and soon ended his moment of victory. It lasted so long that it frightened even me. As to his cousin, she wept violently, though she said nothing. I held him until the attack ended. Then he pushed me away, and leaned his head down silently. Cathy took a seat opposite, and looked into the fire.

'How do you feel now, Master Heathcliff?' I asked after about ten minutes.

'I wish she felt as I do!' he replied, 'Cruel, unkind thing!'

He continued to complain for a quarter of an hour.

'I'm sorry I hurt you, Linton,' his cousin said at last. 'But I wouldn't have been hurt by that little push, and I didn't imagine that you would have been. It wasn't much, was it?'

'I can't speak to you,' he murmured. 'You've hurt me so much that I shall lie awake all night with this cough.' And he began to weep.

'Must I go then?' asked Cathy sadly.

'Leave me alone.'

She waited a long time. He neither looked up nor spoke. At last she made a movement to the door, and I followed. We were brought back by a shout. Linton had slid from his seat on to the floor, and lay twisting himself about, determined to be as annoying as possible. Cathy knelt down and cried.

'I shall lift him up onto the seat,' I said, 'and he may roll about as much as he pleases. We can't stop to watch him. I hope you are satisfied, Miss Cathy, that you are not the person to improve his health.'

She offered him water. He refused the drink, but he would not let her leave him. She sang him a number of songs, and so they went on until the clock struck twelve.

'And tomorrow, Cathy, will you be here tomorrow?' Linton asked, holding her dress as she rose to go.

She whispered in his ear, and at last we left.

'You won't go tomorrow, miss?' I began, as soon as we were out of the house.

She smiled.

'I'll take good care,' I continued. 'I'll have the lock on that door mended.'

'I can get over the wall,' she said, laughing. 'The Grange isn't a prison, and besides, I'm almost seventeen. I'm certain Linton would recover more quickly if he had me to look after him.'

'Listen, miss,' I replied. 'If you attempt going to Wuthering Heights again, I shall inform Mr Linton.'

We reached home before our dinnertime. My master asked no explanation of our absence. He thought we had been wandering in the park. As soon as I entered, I hurried to change my wet shoes, but sitting for such a long time at the Heights had done me harm, and the next morning I was ill. For three weeks I was in bed, unable to carry out my duties.

My little mistress was very kind to me during this lonely time. The moment she left her father's room, she appeared at my bedside. Her day was divided between us. She paid no attention to her meals, her study or her play.

It is true that my master went to sleep early, and I generally needed nothing after six o'clock. I never considered what Cathy did with herself after tea. And though frequently, when she looked in to say goodnight, I noticed a fresh colour in her cheeks, instead of thinking it the result of a cold ride on the moors I imagined it was from a hot fire in the library.

◆

At last I was able to leave my room and move about the house. The first time I sat up in the evening, I asked Cathy to read to me because my eyes were weak. She did so without any pleasure, and after half an hour began to question me: 'Ellen, aren't you tired? Hadn't you better lie down now?'

'No, no, dear, I'm not tired,' I answered, several times.

She then opened her own mouth sleepily and stretched herself, rubbing her eyes and looking at her watch. Finally, she went to her room.

The next night she seemed more impatient still, and on the third she complained of a headache and left me. I thought her behaviour strange, and having remained alone for some time, went up to see if she was feeling better. I could discover no Cathy, upstairs or down. The servants had not seen her, and all was silent in Mr Edgar's room. I returned to my young lady's room, put out my candle, and seated myself at the window.

The moon shone brightly, and I asked myself if she had decided to walk around the garden. I saw a figure creeping along the inner fence of the park, but this was one of the servants. He stood watching the road through the grounds for some time, then suddenly disappeared, to reappear later leading Miss Cathy's horse, and there she was, having just got down and walking by its side.

She entered the sitting room by the long window, and came noiselessly upstairs to her room. She closed the door gently, slipped off her snowy shoes, untied her hat, and was about to remove her outdoor clothes when I suddenly stood up and showed myself. She froze with surprise.

'My dear Miss Cathy,' I began, 'where have you been riding at this time of night? And why should you try to deceive me by telling lies?'

'To the bottom of the park,' she said, uncomfortably.

'And nowhere else?'

'No,' was the reply, in a low voice.

'Oh, Cathy,' I cried sorrowfully, 'you know you have been doing wrong. I'd rather be ill for three months than hear you tell a lie!'

She ran forward and, bursting into tears, threw her arms around my neck.

'Well, Ellen, I'm so afraid of your being angry,' she said. 'Promise that you won't be, and you shall know the truth. I hate to hide it. I've been to Wuthering Heights. I had to keep my promise to Linton. I got possession of the key when the door in the park was being locked again, and I've hardly missed a day since you fell ill. It wasn't to amuse myself that I went. I was often miserable all the time. Now and then I was happy: once in a week, perhaps.

'On my second visit Linton seemed in good spirits. We laughed and talked quite happily for an hour. Then I got tired of sitting, and suggested a game. He agreed to play ball with me. I won every time, and then he became unpleasant again, and coughed, and returned to his chair. He easily recovered his good temper when I sang some pretty songs. That night I came riding home as light as air.

'The next night, Hareton met me and took my horse in. I told him to leave my horse alone. He moved off and, looking up at the letters in stone over the front door, said with a stupid mixture of awkwardness and pride, "Miss Cathy, I can read that now."

'"Wonderful," I exclaimed, "let me hear you – you are getting clever!"

'He slowly spelt out the name, "Hareton Earnshaw".

'"And the figures?" I cried, encouragingly.

'"I cannot tell them yet," he answered.

'I laughed loudly, and told him to walk away, as I had come to see Linton, not him. He became red in the face, and went off annoyed. I suppose he thought himself as educated as Linton!'

'Miss Cathy, dear,' I interrupted, 'you should remember that Hareton is as much your cousin as Master Linton, and you should respect his desire to learn. You made him ashamed of his ignorance before, and he tried to cure it to please you. If you had been brought up as he has, would you have been any better? He was as quick and intelligent a child as you ever were.'

'But wait, Ellen, and hear the rest.

'I entered. Linton was lying on the high-backed seat in the kitchen, and said that he was ill. He asked me to read to him for a bit, and I was going to begin when Hareton pushed the door open, seized Linton by the arm, and swung him off the seat.

'"Get to your own room," he said, in a voice of fury. "Take her there, if she comes to see you. You shan't keep me out of this place!"

'He swore, and nearly threw Linton out. I followed, dropping my book. He kicked it after me, and shut us out.

'Linton stood there white and trembling. He was not pretty then, Ellen. His eyes were full of an expression of mad, powerless fury. He shook the handle of the door. It was locked. He shouted out the most furious threats.

'I took hold of his hands, and tried to pull him away. In the end his cries were stopped by a terrible fit of coughing. Blood rushed from his mouth, and he fell to the ground. I ran into the yard, calling for Zillah. Meanwhile Hareton carried Linton upstairs. Joseph locked the door, and all three of them said I must go home.

'Hareton appeared again, a little way along the roadside. "Miss Cathy," he began "I'm sorry—"

'I struck him with my whip, and rode off.

'I didn't go the Heights the next evening. I had a fear that

Linton was dead. On the third day, I took courage and went. I found him, to my great joy, lying on a bed in a small, tidy room upstairs, reading one of my books. He would neither speak to me nor look at me for an hour, Ellen. And when he did open his mouth, it was to blame me, not Hareton, for what had happened! I got up and left the room, determined to visit him no more.

'It was so miserable going to bed, and getting up, and never hearing anything about him, that I could not stay away and, two days later, I rode over there. I told him that as he thought I came to hurt him, I had now come to say goodbye, and he must tell his father so.

'"You are so much happier than I, Cathy," he said, "that you ought to be better. Sometimes I *am* worthless and bad-tempered. But believe me, if I could be as sweet, kind, and good as you are, I would be. Your kindness has made me love you more deeply than if I deserved your love, and though I can't help showing my nature to you, I shall be sorry until I die!"

'I felt he spoke the truth, and I forgave him.

'About three times since then, we have been happy and hopeful. The rest of my visits have been dull and unhappy, partly from his selfishness and bad nature, partly from his sufferings. I've learned to bear them all. Mr Heathcliff purposely avoids me. I have hardly seen him.

'Now, Ellen, you've heard everything. You'll not tell Papa, will you?'

I thought the matter over, and then went straight to my master's room and told him the whole story. Mr Linton was anxious and upset. Cathy learned that her visits were to end. She wept, but without success. All she got to comfort her was a promise that her father would write and give her cousin permission to come to the Grange when he pleased. Perhaps, if he had realized his nephew's true nature and state of health, details of which I had kept from him, he would not have allowed even that.

Chapter 28   A Meeting on the Moors

Cathy was obedient to her father's commands. Her love for him was still the first feeling in her heart. He had spoken to her without anger, and with the deep emotion of one who is about to leave his dearest daughter among dangers and enemies. A few days later, he said to me: 'I wish my nephew would write, Ellen, or call. Tell me, sincerely, what you think of him. Is he changed for the better, or is there hope of improvement as he grows up?'

'He's very delicate, sir,' I replied, 'and hardly likely to reach manhood, but this I can say: he is not like his father, and if Miss Cathy had the misfortune to marry him, he would not be beyond her control.'

Edgar walked to the window and looked out towards Gimmerton church.

'I've often prayed,' he said, 'for the time to come when I would be laid beside my wife over there. But now I'm beginning to fear it. What can I do for Cathy? How can I leave her? I'd not care for one moment that Linton is Heathcliff's son, if he could comfort her for my loss. But if he should be unworthy – only a weak slave to his father – I cannot leave her to him!'

Spring arrived, but my master gained no real strength. He began once more his walks in the grounds with his daughter and, to her inexperienced eye, the colour in his cheeks and the brightness in his eyes were signs of a return to health.

He wrote once more to his nephew, expressing his desire to see him, and if the sick boy had been really fit to go out so far, I've no doubt his father would have allowed him to come. As it was, Linton replied saying that Mr Heathcliff objected to his visiting the Grange, but that he himself hoped to meet his uncle on his walks, and his cousin too.

Edgar, though he sympathized with the boy, could not at that time of year agree to his request, because he himself could not be

Cathy's companion. When summer came, and June still found him losing strength, he was at last persuaded to let the cousins ride or walk together, about once a week, under my protection. Though he had saved a yearly part of his income so that Cathy would have enough money when he died, he had a natural desire that she might keep, or at least return in a short time to, her old family home, and he considered her only chance of doing that was by a marriage with the young man who was going to own it.

He had no idea that his nephew was failing in health almost as fast as himself; nor had anyone, I believe. No doctor visited the Heights, and no one saw Master Heathcliff to report his condition to us. I myself began to imagine that my fears were false, and that he must actually be growing stronger, when he suggested riding and walking on the moors. I did not realize how wickedly his father treated him when he saw that his heartless plans were threatened with defeat by death.

It was already past midsummer when Cathy and I set out on her first ride to join her cousin. It was a heavy day, without sunshine. Our meeting place had been fixed where two roads met, but when we arrived there a little farm boy, sent as messenger, told us that Master Heathcliff was just this side of the Heights and would be very grateful if we would go on a little farther.

We found him only a quarter of a mile from his own door. He lay on the ground, waiting for us to come to him, and did not rise until we were within a few yards. He walked with difficulty, and looked very pale.

Cathy looked at him in grief and surprise, and asked whether he was worse than usual.

'No, better − better,' he replied, breathlessly, trembling and holding on to her hand, as if he needed support.

'But you look worse,' repeated his cousin. 'You are thinner and−'

'I'm tired,' he interrupted, hurriedly. 'It's too hot for walking. Let's rest here. I often feel sick. Father says I'm growing too fast.'

Cathy sat down, and he lay beside her. She talked, and he listened. He clearly had great difficulty in keeping up any kind of conversation. His lack of interest in what was said to him, and his lack of power to amuse her in any way, were so clear that she could not hide her disappointment.

A change had come over his whole person and manner. The unpleasant look had given place to a dull weakness: there was less childish temper and more of the self-pitying low spirits of a continually sick person. Cathy noticed as well as I did that he felt it a punishment, rather than a pleasure, to suffer our company, and she was quick to suggest, a little later, that she should leave.

This suggestion, unexpectedly, excited Linton and threw him into a strange state of fear. He looked anxiously towards the Heights, begging that she would remain another half-hour at least.

'Stay to rest yourself,' he said. 'And, Cathy, don't think or say that I am very unwell. It's the heavy weather and heat that makes me dull. I walked around, before you came, a great deal. Tell Uncle I'm in rather good health, will you?'

'I'll tell him that *you* say so,' replied my young lady, uncertainly.

'And be here again next Thursday,' he continued, avoiding her strange look. 'And – and, if you *do* meet my father, don't let him suppose that I've been silent and stupid. Don't look sad, or he'll be angry.'

'Is he severe to you now, Master Heathcliff?' I inquired.

Linton looked at me, but he did not answer. After another ten minutes, during which his head fell sleepily on his breast, and he did nothing but complain of tiredness or pain, Cathy began to pick berries to amuse herself.

'Why did he wish to see me?' she asked, in a low voice. 'It's just as if it were a duty he was forced to do, for fear that his father would be angry with him. But I'm not here to give Mr Heathcliff pleasure.'

Linton suddenly awoke.

'I thought I heard my father!' he exclaimed. 'Be quiet! He's coming.' And he held on to Cathy's arm.

Cathy freed herself and called to her horse.

'I'll be here next Thursday,' she cried, jumping up. 'Goodbye. Quick, Ellen.'

When we reached home, my master requested an account of the meeting. Both Cathy and I said little: Cathy, because she thought that her cousin was pretending as usual that his sufferings were greater than they were, and I, because I hardly knew what to hide, and what to tell.

Chapter 29   The Trap

Seven days passed, every one marking its passing by the rapid worsening of Edgar Linton's condition. We would have kept the truth from Cathy, but her own quick intelligence guessed what was coming. When Thursday came round, she could not bear to mention her ride. I did so, and obtained permission to order her out of doors, since her father's sick room had become her whole world and she spent every moment by his side. Her face had become pale with watching and sorrow, and my master gladly sent her off to what he imagined to be a happy change of scene.

He had a fixed idea that as his nephew was like him in appearance, he must be like him in mind, because Linton's letters, written, no doubt, under his father's eyes, gave few signs of his real character. Through understandable weakness, I did not correct this belief, asking myself what good there would be in disturbing my master's last days with information he was powerless to use.

Cathy's poor little heart was sad as we set out in the afternoon.

Linton was waiting in the same place as before. There was more life in his manner of receiving us this time, but not the life of high spirits nor of joy. It looked to me more like fear.

'It's late,' he said, speaking sharply and with difficulty. 'Is your father very ill? I thought you wouldn't come.'

Cathy's greeting froze on her lips.

'My father *is* very ill,' she said. 'Why didn't you send to free me from my promise, if you wished I wouldn't keep it? Come! I want an explanation. Playing and nonsense are completely driven out of my mind now; I've no time for pretence.'

Linton shivered, and looked at her, half ashamed.

'Pretence!' he said, in a low voice. 'Please, Cathy, don't look so angry. Scorn me as much as you please; I'm worthless, but I'm too weak for your anger – hate my father, and not me!'

'Nonsense!' cried Cathy, angrily. 'He's trembling, as if I were going to touch him! Get off! Let go of my dress!'

With tears pouring down his face, Linton had thrown himself on the ground. He seemed helpless with terror.

'Oh!' he wept, 'I can't bear it! Cathy, I am behaving falsely to you, too, and I dare not tell you now! But leave me, and I shall be killed! Dear Cathy, my life is in your hands! You have said you loved me, so perhaps you *will* agree – and he'll let me die with you!'

My young lady was thoroughly upset and afraid. She bent to raise him up.

'Agree to what?' she asked. 'To stay? Explain the meaning of this talk. Tell me at once what is weighing on your heart. You wouldn't do me any harm, would you? You wouldn't let anyone hurt your best friend, if you could prevent it?'

'But my father threatened me,' cried the boy with difficulty. 'I *dare* not tell.'

'Keep your secret, then,' said Cathy, with scornful pity. 'Save yourself; I'm not afraid.'

I heard a movement, and saw Heathcliff. He didn't look at my companions but, calling to me in an almost friendly way, said: 'It is something to see you so near my house, Nelly. How are they at the Grange?' he added, in a lower voice. 'It is said that Edgar Linton is on his deathbed: perhaps that's not true?'

'No, my master is dying,' I replied. 'It is true enough.'

'How long will he last, do you think?' he asked.

'I don't know.'

'Because,' he continued, looking at the two young people, 'that boy seems determined to defeat me. I'd thank his uncle to be quick and go before him.'

'I would say,' I remarked, 'that instead of wandering on the hills, he ought to be in bed, in the care of a doctor.'

'Get up, Linton!' he shouted. 'Don't twist about on the ground – up, this moment!'

Linton had sunk down again, in helpless fear, when his father looked at him. He tried several times to obey, but his strength failed him.

'I will, Father,' he said breathlessly. 'But leave me alone – I've done as you wished, I'm sure. Ah! Stay with me, Cathy. Give me your hand.'

'Take mine,' said his father, 'and stand on your feet. There, now. You would imagine I was cruel to him, Miss Cathy, to excite such terror. Be kind enough to walk home with him: he trembles if I touch him.'

'I can't go to Wuthering Heights,' said Cathy. 'My father has forbidden it. Linton, dear, your father won't harm you. Why are you so afraid?'

'Very well,' answered Heathcliff, 'we'll respect Cathy's decision. Come then, my brave boy! Are you willing to return in my company?'

He made a movement to seize the boy, but Linton, stepping back, held on to his cousin, and begged her in such a miserable manner to go with him that she could not refuse him. What frightened him, we could not imagine. We reached the door. Cathy walked in, and I stood waiting until she led the sick boy to a chair, expecting her to come straight out again.

Mr Heathcliff pushed me forward, made me sit down, and then turned and locked the door.

'I am by myself, and would like a little company,' he said. 'You shall have some tea. Hareton has gone with some cattle to the fields, and Zillah and Joseph are also out. Miss Linton, I give you what I have, though the present is hardly worth accepting. It is Linton I mean. Take your seat next to him.'

Cathy stepped close to Heathcliff, her dark eyes flashing.

'I'm not afraid of you,' she said. 'Give me that key! I wouldn't eat or drink here if I were dying of hunger!'

Heathcliff looked up with a sort of surprise at her anger; or possibly reminded by her voice and expression of the person from whom she got it. She had half succeeded in getting the key from his loosened fingers, when he recovered it.

'Now, Catherine Linton,' he said, 'stand back, or I shall knock you down.'

Taking no notice of his warning, she seized his closed hand, and finding that her nails had no effect, dug her teeth in rather sharply. Heathcliff gave me a look that prevented me from speaking for a moment. He opened his fingers suddenly, seized her, and gave her a number of blows on both sides of the head.

I rushed at him furiously.

'You devil!' I began.

A push on my chest silenced me. I am overweight and soon get out of breath. With the blow, and with fury, I fell back unsteadily, my lungs feeling ready to burst.

The scene was over in two minutes. Cathy, freed, put her two hands to her head. She trembled, poor thing, and leaned against the table in complete confusion.

'I know how to punish children, you see,' said the heartless man. 'Go to Linton now, as I told you, and cry as you like. I shall be your father tomorrow – all the father you'll have in a few days – and you will be punished again and again if you need it.'

Cathy ran to me instead of Linton, and knelt down and put her burning cheek on my knee, weeping aloud. Her cousin had moved back into a corner of his seat, as quiet as a mouse – pleased, I dare say, that punishment had been given not to him, but another. Heathcliff rose and made tea. He poured it out and handed me a cup.

'Wash away your anger,' he said, 'and help your own naughty pet and mine. I'm going to find your horses.'

Our first thought, when he left, was to force a way out. The kitchen door was locked outside and the windows were too narrow even for Cathy's little figure.

'Master Linton,' I cried, seeing that we could not escape, 'you know what your wicked father intends to do, and you shall tell us.'

'Yes, Linton,' said Cathy. 'It was for you I came, and it will be ungrateful if you refuse.'

'Give me some tea, I'm thirsty; then I'll tell you,' he answered. 'Mrs Dean, go away. I don't like you standing over me. Now, Cathy, you are letting your tears fall into my cup! I won't drink that. Give me another.'

Cathy pushed another to him, and dried her eyes. I was displeased by the miserable boy's calmness, since he was no longer in terror himself. His wild anxiety had disappeared as soon as we entered the Heights, so I guessed that he had been threatened with a terrible punishment if he failed to trick us into coming.

'Father wants us to be married,' he explained, after drinking some of the liquid. 'And he's afraid that I shall die if we wait, so we are to be married in the morning, and you are to stay here tonight.'

'*You* marry?' I exclaimed. 'Why – do you imagine that beautiful young lady, that healthy active girl, will tie herself to a little monkey like you?'

'Stay all night!' said Cathy, looking slowly round. 'Ellen, I'll burn the door down and get out.'

Linton was frightened again for his dear self.

'Won't you have me, and save me? Oh sweetest Cathy, you mustn't go and leave me! You *must* obey my father, you *must*!'

'I must obey my own,' she replied, 'and save him from this cruel anxiety. The whole night! What would he think! Be quiet! You're in no danger!'

Heathcliff now re-entered.

'Your animals have wandered off,' he said. 'Now, Linton, go to your room. Zillah won't be here tonight, so you must undress yourself.'

He held the door open, and his son rushed out like a frightened little dog. The door was locked again.

Heathcliff came closer to the fire, where my mistress and I stood silently. Cathy looked up and raised her hand to her cheek. Anyone else would have found it impossible to see this childish act with severity, but he looked fiercely at her and said: 'Oh, you aren't afraid of me? Your courage is well hidden!'

'I *am* afraid now,' she replied, 'because if I stay, my father will be miserable. Mr Heathcliff, let me go home! I promise to marry Linton. Papa would like me to, and I love him. Why should you force me to do what I'll do of my own free will?'

'Let him dare to force you!' I cried. 'There's law in the land, thank God, though we live in an out-of-the-way place.'

'Silence!' said the wicked man. 'I don't want *you* to speak! Miss Linton, I shall enjoy myself greatly in thinking that your father will be miserable. As to your promise to marry Linton, you will not leave this place until it is carried out.'

'Send Ellen, then, to let Papa know I'm safe!' exclaimed Cathy, weeping. 'Ellen, he'll think we are lost. What shall we do?'

'Not he! He'll think you were tired of looking after him, and ran off for a little amusement,' answered Heathcliff. 'You must admit that you entered my house of your own free will, in disobedience of his wishes. Weep as much as you like! It's nothing to me!'

'Mr Heathcliff, if Father thought I had left him on purpose, and if he died before I returned, how could I bear to live? I'm going to kneel here before you. You can't help pitying me!'

Heathcliff pushed her away with a curse. I was going to tell him what I thought of his behaviour, but I was silenced in the middle of a sentence by a threat that I would be shown into a room by myself, the next word I spoke.

It was getting dark. We heard a sound of voices at the gate. Our host hurried out immediately: *he* was quick to understand and act; *we* were not. There was talk for two or three minutes, and he returned alone.

'I thought it was your cousin Hareton,' I said to Cathy. 'Who knows – perhaps he might help you.'

'It was three servants sent to search for you from the Grange,' said Heathcliff. 'You should have opened the window and called out.'

At learning of this chance that we had missed, we both wept uncontrollably. He allowed us to weep on until nine o'clock, when he ordered us to go upstairs to Zillah's room.

Neither of us lay down. Cathy took up her position by the narrow window and watched for morning. I seated myself on a chair and blamed myself for failing in my duty.

At seven o'clock Heathcliff called Cathy out. I rose to follow, but he turned the key again.

'Be patient,' he said. 'I'll send up your breakfast.' And he left me still a prisoner in the room.

After two or three hours I heard a footstep. Hareton entered, bearing enough food for me all day.

'Stay one minute!' I began.

'No,' he cried, and went away.

And there I remained the whole day, and the whole of the next night; and another, and another. Five nights and four days I remained there, seeing nobody but Hareton, once every morning, and he was silent and paid no attention to any attempt to move him to pity.

Chapter 30   Mr Green Is Too Late

On the fifth morning, or rather afternoon, I heard a different step – lighter and shorter – and Zillah entered the room.

'Oh, my dear Mrs Dean,' she exclaimed. 'Well! There is talk about you in Gimmerton. I thought you were drowned in a pool, and Miss Cathy with you, until master told me you'd been found and he'd given you shelter here. And how long were you in the water? How are you feeling? Did master save you, Mrs Dean?'

'Your master is a true devil!' I replied.

'What do you mean?' asked Zillah. 'It's not his story: it's what they say in the village. When the master heard it, he just smiled and said the water had got into your head and made you a little mad, so he kept you safe until you recovered. He told me to unlock the door and tell you to go to the Grange, and to carry a message from him that your young lady will follow in time to attend your master's funeral.'

'Mr Edgar isn't dead?' I exclaimed. 'Oh! Zillah!'

'No, no. Sit down a moment, you're still sick from the accident, poor thing! He's not dead. The doctor thinks he may last one more day. I met him on the road and asked.'

I seized my outdoor things and hurried downstairs. There was no one around to tell me where Cathy might be. The place was full of sunshine and the door stood wide open. I stood there for a moment, when a slight cough drew my attention. Linton lay on a seat, sucking a stick of sugar.

'Where is Miss Cathy?' I demanded.

He sucked on like a baby.

'Has she gone?' I asked.

'No,' he replied. 'She's upstairs. She's not to go. We won't let her.'

'You won't let her!' I exclaimed. 'Direct me to her room immediately!'

'Father says I'm not to be soft with Cathy,' he answered. 'She's my wife, and it's shameful she should wish to leave me. He says she wants me to die so that she may have all my money, but she can't have it and she can't go home. She may cry and be sick as much as she pleases.'

He started on his sugar again, and closed his eyes.

'Master Heathcliff,' I went on, 'have you forgotten all Cathy's kindness to you last winter, when you said you loved her, and she brought you books, and sang you songs, and came to see you, in spite of bad weather? And now you believe what your father says, and join him against her!'

The corner of Linton's mouth fell, and he took the sweet from his lips.

'I can't stay with her,' he said. 'She cries so much that I can't bear it. She complains all night, and I can't sleep.'

'Is Mr Heathcliff out?' I inquired.

'He's in the yard,' he replied, 'talking to the doctor, who says that Uncle is dying at last. I'm glad, because I shall be master of the Grange after him – and Cathy always spoke of it as her house! It's mine: Papa says everything she has is mine. She offered me all her nice books, and her pretty birds, and her horse, if I would get the key of our room and let her out, but I told her she had nothing to give – they were mine, all mine. And then she cried, and took a little picture from her neck, two pictures in a gold case – on one side her mother, and on the other, Uncle, when they were young. I said they were mine, too, and tried to get them from her. The nasty thing pushed me off and hurt me. But when she heard Father coming she was afraid, and divided the case, and gave me her mother's picture and tried to hide the other, but Father took the one from me, and crushed the other under his foot, and struck Cathy down.'

'And were you pleased?' I asked.

'I didn't look,' he said. 'I shut my eyes every time my father strikes anything, he does it so hard. But she deserved punishing for pushing me. But when he had gone, she showed me her cheek cut on the inside, and collected up the bits of the picture, and has not spoken to me since. Perhaps she can't speak, because of the pain. I don't like to think so.'

'Can you get the key?' I asked.

'Yes, when I'm upstairs, but I can't walk upstairs now.'

'Which room is she in?'

'Oh, I shan't tell you that! It is our secret.'

He turned his face on to his arm, and shut his eyes again.

I considered it best to leave without seeing Mr Heathcliff, and to bring help for my young lady from the Grange. When I arrived home, my fellow servants were very surprised to see me, and happy to hear that their little mistress was safe.

I hurried to Edgar Linton's door.

How changed I found him, even in those few days! He thought of Cathy, and murmured her name.

'Cathy is coming, dear master,' I whispered. 'She is alive and well, and will be here, I hope, tonight.'

He half rose up, looked eagerly round the room, and then fell back unconscious. When he had recovered, I told him what had happened, and the reason for it. I said as little as possible against Linton, and I did not describe all his father's cruel behaviour.

He guessed that one of his enemy's purposes was to get hold of his money, as well as the land and house, for his son, or rather for himself. But my master could not understand why he did not wait for his death, having no idea how ill his nephew really was. He felt, though, that his will had better be changed. Instead of leaving Cathy's money in her own hands, he decided to put it in the care of some responsible people for her use during her life, and for her children if she had any, after her death. By that means, it could not pass to Heathcliff if Linton died.

I sent a man to fetch the lawyer, and four more, with suitable weapons, to the Heights, to demand the return of Cathy. Both parties were a long time returning. The first man returned to say that Mr Green had been out, and when he came would have a little business to do in the village, but he would be at the Grange before morning. The four men also came back without my mistress. They brought word that Cathy was ill and could not leave her room. I cursed the stupid men for believing such a story, and decided to go myself, at dawn, with a whole lot of men, and get her.

Happily I was saved the journey. At three o'clock in the morning I heard a knock at the door. Thinking it was the lawyer, I went down myself to admit him. My own sweet little mistress fell on my neck, weeping and crying: 'Ellen! Ellen! Is Papa still alive?'

I couldn't bear to be present at their meeting. After a quarter of an hour, I went in. Cathy's misery was as silent as her father's joy. He died, kissing her cheek.

Cathy remained by the deathbed until I managed to persuade her to come away and take some rest. At dinnertime the lawyer appeared, too late. He had called at Wuthering Heights and sold himself to Heathcliff, which was the cause of his delay.

He made himself busy ordering everything and everybody around the place. All the servants except myself were dismissed, and the funeral was hurried over. Cathy, Mrs Linton Heathcliff now, was allowed to stay at the Grange until her father's body had been laid side by side with her mother's, on the edge of the moor.

◆

The evening after the funeral, my young lady and I were seated in the library. Cathy had told me of how she had at last persuaded Linton to help her to escape. We had just agreed that the best thing that could happen to her would be to have permission to go on living at the Grange, at least during Linton's lifetime – he being allowed to join her there, and I to remain as housekeeper – when one of the dismissed servants who had not yet left, rushed in to say that Heathcliff was coming through the yard.

He made no ceremony of knocking or sending in his name. He was master, and walked straight in, without saying a word.

It was the same room into which he had been shown, as a guest, eighteen years before. Time had changed his appearance very little. He was the same man, his dark face rather more under control, his body a little heavier, perhaps. Cathy had risen, with the idea of rushing out, when she saw him.

'Stop!' he said, holding her by the arm. 'No more running away! I've come to fetch you home, and I hope you'll be an obedient daughter, and not encourage my son to further disobedience. He's suffered for that, I can tell you.'

'Why not let Cathy continue here,' I begged, 'and send Master Linton to her?'

'I'm looking for a tenant for the Grange,' he answered, 'and I want my children with me. Besides, that girl owes me her services for her food and room. I'm not going to keep her in laziness and rich living. Hurry and get ready.'

'I shall,' said Catherine. 'Linton is all I have to love in the world, and though you have done what you could to make us hate each other, you cannot succeed!'

'It is not I who will make him hateful to you – it is his own spirit. He's bitter about your going off, and I heard him draw a pleasant picture of what he would do to you if he were stronger.'

'I know he has a bad nature,' said Cathy. 'He's your son. But I'm glad that mine is better, to forgive it. And I know that he loves me, and for that reason I love him. Mr Heathcliff, *you* have *nobody* to love you. You *are* miserable, aren't you?'

'You will be sorry for yourself soon,' said Heathcliff, 'if you stand there another minute. Go and get your things.'

She went, and in her absence I began to beg for Zillah's place at the Heights but he would not agree. He told me to be silent and then, for the first time, looked round the room and at the pictures.

Having studied the painting of Mrs Linton, he said: 'I shall have that at home. Not because I need it, but . . .'

He turned quickly to the fire and, with a strange smile, continued, 'I'll tell you what I did yesterday! I got the man who was digging Edgar Linton's grave to remove the earth from *her* coffin lid and I opened it. It is still her face, but the gravedigger said it would change if the air blew on it, so I covered it again. Then I broke off one side of the coffin – not on her husband's side, curse him! – and I paid the man to break off one side of mine, the side nearest to her, when I'm laid there beside her.'

'You were very wicked, Mr Heathcliff,' I exclaimed. 'Weren't you ashamed to play such games with the dead?'

'Play games with her? No! *She* has been playing games with *me*, night and day, for eighteen years – without pause, without pity – until last night; and last night I was at peace. I dreamed I was sleeping the last sleep beside that sleeper, with my heart stopped and my cheek frozen against hers.

'It began strangely, that feeling,' he went on. 'You know I was wild after she died, and always, day after day, praying her spirit to return to me. I have a strong belief in ghosts. I am certain that they can and do exist among us! The day she was buried, there came a fall of snow. In the evening, I went to the churchyard. It was bitterly cold and, being alone, I said to myself, "I'll have her in my arms again!" I got a spade and began to dig. I had reached the coffin, and was on the point of opening it, when it seemed that I heard a murmur from someone above, close to the edge of the grave and, bending down, I thought, "If only I can get this off, I wish they would cover us both over with the earth." There was another murmur close to my ear. I appeared to feel warm breath. I knew that no living thing of flesh and blood was near, but I felt with complete certainty that Cathy was there, not under me, but on the earth. A sudden sense of happiness flowed through my heart, through every part of my body. I was indescribably comforted. Her presence was with me while I refilled the grave, and it led me home. You may laugh if you will, but I was sure I would see her there! The door was locked − that fool Hindley and my wife tried to stop me entering. I remember stopping to kick him, and then hurrying upstairs. I looked round impatiently − I felt her by me − I could almost see her, but I could not! And, since then, sometimes more and sometimes less, I've suffered from that unbearable misery! When I sat in the house, it seemed that if I went out I would meet her; when on the moors, that I would meet her coming in. She *must* be somewhere at the Heights, I was certain! And when I slept in her room, the moment I closed my eyes, she was either outside the window, or entering the room, or even resting her dear body on the same bed as she did as a child. I opened my eyes a hundred times a night − always to be disappointed! For eighteen years she was killing me slowly, with the ghost of a hope. Now, since I've seen her, I'm at peace − a little.'

Mr Heathcliff paused, and dried his forehead. His eyes were fixed on the fire; the expression on his face was strangely troubled, but less severe than usual. He only half addressed me, and I kept silent. After a short period, he looked once again at the picture, took it down, and leaned it against a chair.

As he was doing so, Cathy entered, announcing that she was ready when her horse was.

'Send the picture over tomorrow,' said Heathcliff to me. Then, turning to her, he added, 'You can do without your horse. Your own feet will serve you. Come along.'

'Goodbye, Ellen,' whispered my dear mistress. 'Come and see me.'

'Take care you do no such thing,' said her new father.

And, fixing Cathy's arm under his own, he hurried her away.

Chapter 31   Proud as a Princess

It was only last summer that Miss Cathy was married. I have paid a visit to the Heights, but I have not seen her since she went. Joseph would not let me enter, saying that she was not well and the master was not in. Zillah has told me something of the way in which they live. She thinks Cathy proud, and doesn't like her.

'The first thing she did,' Zillah said, 'on her arrival, was to run upstairs without even wishing Joseph and myself good evening. She shut herself up in Linton's room, and remained until morning. Then, while the master and Hareton were at breakfast, she entered and asked if the doctor could be sent for, as her cousin was very ill.

'"We know that," answered Heathcliff, "but his life is worth nothing, and I won't spend anything on him."

'"But I can't tell what to do," she said, "and if no one will help me, he'll die!"

'"Leave us!" cried the master. "No one here cares what happens to him. If you do, act the nurse; if you don't, lock him up and leave him."

'Then she began to ask me for help, and I said I'd had enough trouble with the boy. We each had our work to do, and hers was to look after Linton.

'How they managed, I don't know. He seemed to be complaining day and night, and she had very little rest, judging by her white face and heavy eyes. She sometimes came into the kitchen as if she would beg for help, but I never dare disobey the master, Mrs Dean, and it was no business of mine. I did pity her, I'm sure, but I didn't want to lose my post, you know.

'At last, one night, she came into my room, saying, "Tell Mr Heathcliff that his son is dying. Get up now and tell him!"

'She disappeared. I lay for a quarter of an hour, but heard nothing.

'"She's mistaken," I said to myself.

'My sleep was disturbed a second time by a sharp ringing of Linton's bell. The master called me to see what was the matter. I gave him Cathy's message.

'In a few minutes he came out with a lighted candle and went to their room. Mrs Heathcliff was seated by the bedside. Mr Heathcliff went up, held the light to Linton's dead face, and touched him. Afterwards, he turned to Cathy.

'"Now," he said, "how do you feel?"

'"He's safe, and I'm free; but you have left me to struggle so long against death, alone, that I feel and see only death."

'I gave her a little wine. Hareton and Joseph, woken by the noise, entered. Joseph was glad of the boy's removal, I think. Hareton seemed a bit upset, though he was more occupied with staring at Cathy.

'In the morning she said she was ill. She stayed upstairs for two weeks.'

Zillah visited her twice a day, and would have been rather more friendly, but her attempts at increasing kindness were proudly refused.

Heathcliff went up once, to show her Linton's will. He had left the whole of his, and what had been her money, to his father. The miserable boy was persuaded, or threatened, into that act during her week's absence, when his uncle died. He could not change the lands, being under age, but Mr Heathcliff has claimed and kept them in his wife's right, and his own also. I suppose that since Cathy has no friends or money to support her case, she can do nothing about this.

'Nobody,' Zillah went on, 'ever went near her door, except on that one occasion, other than myself. The first time she came down was a Sunday afternoon. She said she could not bear the cold upstairs any longer. Heathcliff had gone off to Thrushcross Grange, and Joseph was at church. I told Hareton his cousin would probably sit with us. He became red in the face, and passed his eyes over his hands and clothes. I saw he wanted to look respectable, so, laughing, I offered to help him. He was uncertain at first, but I talked him into accepting my help.

'The mistress walked in, as cold as ice and as proud as a princess. I got up and offered her my seat in the armchair. No, she turned up her nose at my politeness. Hareton rose too, asking her to come and sit close to the fire. She got a chair for herself, and placed it at a distance from both of us.

'Having sat until she was warm, she began to look around and discovered a number of books on a shelf. They were too high up for her to reach, and her cousin, after watching for a while, at last found the courage to help her.

'She didn't thank him, but she had accepted his help, and he was brave enough to stand behind as she examined the books, and even to point out what pleased him best in certain old pictures. Nor was he discouraged by the sharp manner in which she drew the page away from his finger. He was happy to look at her instead of the book. His attention, by degrees, became fixed on the study of her thick, silky hair. He couldn't see her face, and she couldn't see him. And, like a child, he went on from staring to touching. He put out his hand and passed it over one curl as gently as if it were a bird. If he had stuck a knife into her neck, she could not have turned on him in such a fury.

'"Get away this moment! How dare you touch me! I can't bear you!"

'Hareton moved away, looking foolish. He sat down very quietly, and she continued turning over the pages of books. Finally he came over to me and whispered, 'Will you ask her to read to us, Zillah? I should like to hear her.'

'"Mr Hareton wishes you to read to us," I said at once. "He'd be very grateful."

'She looked angry and answered, "The whole set of you will be good enough to understand that I will accept no pretence of kindness from you! When I would have given my life for one kind word, you avoided me. I'm driven down here by the cold, not to amuse you or enjoy your company."

'"But I offered more than once, and asked," said Hareton. "I asked Mr Heathcliff to let me nurse for you when Linton was sick—"

'"Be silent! I'll go out of doors, rather than have your unpleasant voice in my ears!" said my lady.

'The icy weather continued, and she was forced to keep us company more and more. But since then I've been as unfriendly as herself, and she has no one among us who likes her, and she doesn't deserve one.'

On hearing this account from Zillah, I decided to leave my employment, and take a small house, and get Cathy to come and live with me. But Mr Heathcliff would never allow it, and I can see no way out unless she could marry again.

And that, Mr Lockwood, is the present state of affairs at Wuthering Heights.

Told by Mr Lockwood

Chapter 32   I Revisit the Heights

Soon after recovering from my illness last year, I left Thrushcross Grange and returned to London. The loneliness and wildness of the place had not suited me at all, and soon I had almost forgotten my stay there.

But this September I was invited to the north for the shooting season and, on my journey to my friend's property, I unexpectedly came within fifteen miles of Gimmerton. A sudden desire to visit Thrushcross Grange again seized me.

It seemed to me I might as well pass the night under my own roof as at a hotel. Besides, I could easily take a day to arrange matters with my landlord, as I had warned him that when my agreed year as his tenant was at an end in October, I did not intend to keep the house.

I rode into the courtyard at the Grange and saw an old woman sitting on the steps.

'Is Mrs Dean inside?' I asked.

'Mrs Dean? No!' she answered. 'She doesn't live here. She's up at the Heights now.'

I made arrangements for the night, and then climbed the stony road to Mr Heathcliff's home just as the sun was setting.

This time I did not have to unchain the gate, or to knock. A sweet scent of garden flowers hung on the air. The doors and windows were open, and two members of the household, seated just inside, could be both seen and heard. I paused.

A voice, as sweet as a silver bell, was ordering someone else to read some sentences correctly.

A deep male voice began to read. The speaker was a young man, respectably dressed and seated at a table with a book in front of him. His good-looking face shone with pleasure, and his eyes kept wandering impatiently from the page to a small white hand over his shoulder. Its owner stood behind, her light, shining curls touching, now and then, his brown hair, as she bent to examine his studies. It was lucky he could not see her pretty face, or he would never have been so steady.

The lesson was completed, not free from mistakes, but the pupil claimed a reward and received kisses that he generously returned. Then Cathy and Hareton, for it was them that I was watching, came to the door, and from their conversation I judged they were about to go for a walk on the moor. Clearly, an interruption by me would not be welcome.

I went round to find the kitchen. Here, too, the door was open, and at it sat my old friend Nelly Dean, sewing and singing a song, which was often interrupted from inside by the complaining voice of old Joseph.

Mrs Dean jumped to her feet, crying: 'Why, it's Mr Lockwood! How could you think of returning in this way? All's shut up at the Grange.'

'I am leaving again tomorrow,' I answered. 'And how have you come here?'

'Zillah left, and Mr Heathcliff wished me to come, soon after you went to London, sir. Have you walked from Gimmerton?'

'From the Grange. And while they prepare my rooms there, I want to finish my business with your master.'

'What business, sir? He's gone out at present.'

'About the rent.'

'Oh! Then it is with Mrs Heathcliff you must settle, or rather with me. She hasn't learned to manage her affairs yet, and I act for her: there's nobody else.'

I looked surprised.

'Ah! You haven't heard of Heathcliff's death, I see,' she continued.

'Heathcliff dead? How long ago?'

'Three months. Sit down, and I'll tell you all about it. But wait! You've had nothing to eat, have you?'

'I want nothing. I have ordered supper at home. You sit down, too. I never thought of his dying. You don't expect them back for some time – the young people?'

'No, I have to be cross with them every evening about their late wanderings, but they don't listen to me.'

And then she told me about the strange end of Heathcliff.

PART 5   THE FRUIT OF REVENGE IS TASTELESS
(FEBRUARY–APRIL 1802)

Told by Mrs Ellen Dean

Chapter 33   Cathy Is Bored

When, within two weeks of your leaving the Grange, Mr Lockwood, I was sent for to go to Wuthering Heights, I obeyed joyfully, for Cathy. My first meeting with her upset me and filled me with grief: she had changed so much since our separation. Mr Heathcliff did not explain why he had changed his mind about my coming. He only said he was tired of seeing Cathy, so I must make the little room upstairs, which had belonged to Linton, into my sitting room and keep her with me. She seemed pleased with this arrangement and, a little at a time, I secretly brought over from the Grange a number of books and other things.

Cathy was happy enough at first, but after a short time she became restless and difficult to please. For one thing, she was forbidden to move out of the garden. For another, in looking after the house, I was forced to leave her frequently, and she complained of loneliness. She preferred quarrelling with Joseph in the kitchen to sitting in peace by herself. I did not mind this, but Hareton often had to be in the kitchen too. Though at the beginning she either left when he arrived, or quietly joined me in my work, taking no notice of him at all, after a time she changed her behaviour and was unable to leave him alone – she talked about him, remarking on his laziness and stupidity, asking herself how he could bear the life he led.

'He's just like a dog, isn't he, Ellen?' she once remarked, 'or a horse? He does his work, eats his food, and sleeps. Do you ever dream, Hareton? Can't you speak to me?'

She looked at him, but he refused to look at her.

'I know why Hareton never speaks when I am in the kitchen,' she exclaimed on another occasion. 'He's afraid I'll laugh at him. Ellen, what do you think? He began to teach himself to read once, and because I laughed he burned his books and gave it up. Wasn't he a fool?'

'Weren't you naughty?' I said. 'Answer me that.'

'Perhaps I was,' she went on, 'but I didn't expect him to be so silly. Hareton, if I gave you a book, would you take it now?'

She placed one in his hand. He threw it away and threatened her.

'Well, I shall put it in the table drawer,' she said, 'and I'm going to bed.'

She whispered to me to watch whether he touched it when she went out. He would not come near it, to her great disappointment. I saw she was sorry about his continued unfriendliness and knew that it was her fault for frightening him off improving himself.

She tried hard to put right the harm she had done. While I was at work in the kitchen she would bring in some pleasant book and read aloud to me. When Hareton was there, she would pause at some interesting point and leave the book open at the page. She did this repeatedly, but he was determined to ignore it, and in the wet weather he got into the habit of smoking with Joseph, while on fine evenings he went off shooting.

All the time, Cathy complained and worried me to talk to her, and said that her life was useless.

◆

Mr Heathcliff, who found any sort of society less and less desirable, had almost forbidden Hareton to enter his room. The young man, owing to an accident at the beginning of March, had to remain at home in the kitchen for several days. His gun had exploded while he was out on the hills by himself. His arm was hurt, and he had lost a good deal of blood. It suited Cathy to have him by the fireside, or at least made her hate her room upstairs more.

On Easter Monday, Joseph went to Gimmerton market with some cattle, and in the afternoon I was busy ironing clothes in the kitchen. Hareton sat in silence as usual in the chimney corner, and my little mistress was drawing pictures on the windows, and amusing herself by little bursts of song and whispered exclamations and quick looks of impatience in the direction of her cousin, who went on smoking and looking into the fire.

I paid little attention to her actions, but soon I heard her begin: 'I've found out, Hareton, that I want – that I'm glad – that I would like you to be my cousin, now, if you hadn't become so unpleasant to me, and rough.'

Hareton gave no answer.

'Hareton! Hareton! Hareton! Do you hear?'

'Get off with you!' he said fiercely.

'Let me take that pipe,' she said, slowly stretching her hand out, and removing it from his mouth.

Before he could attempt to get it back, it was broken and

thrown in the fire. He swore at her, and seized another.

'Stop!' she cried. 'You must listen to me first, and I can't speak with those clouds floating in my face.'

'Will you go away,' he exclaimed, 'and leave me alone!'

'No,' she replied. 'Come, you must take notice of me. You are my cousin, and must recognize me. When I call you stupid, I don't mean I'm scornful of you.'

'I shall have nothing to do with you, and your cursed making fun of me,' he answered, 'and I'll never look at you again. Move out of the way, now, this minute!'

Cathy went to the window seat, biting her lip and trying not to weep.

'You should be friends with your cousin, Mr Hareton,' I said, 'as she is sorry for her past behaviour. It would do you a great deal of good, to have her for a companion.'

'A companion?' he cried. 'When she hates me, and doesn't think me fit to clean her shoes?'

'It's not I who hate you, it's you who hate me!' Cathy said, now openly weeping. 'You hate me more than Mr Heathcliff does.'

'That's not true,' began Hareton. 'Why then have I made him angry, by defending you a hundred times – and even when you laughed at me, and scorned me!'

'I didn't know you defended me,' she answered, drying her eyes, 'and I was angry and bitter at everybody. But now I thank you, and beg you to forgive me.'

She came to the fire, and offered her hand. His face grew as dark as a thundercloud, and he would not see it or take it.

Cathy must have guessed that it was pride, and not dislike, that caused the refusal because, after remaining a moment undecided, she bent down and gave his cheek a gentle kiss. The naughty thing thought I had not seen her and, moving away, took her former seat by the window. I shook my head disapprovingly, and she went red.

Hareton was very careful, for some minutes, that his face should not be seen, and when he did raise it, he did not know where to turn his eyes.

Cathy passed the time in wrapping a fine book neatly in white paper and, having tied it with string, and addressed it to 'Mr Hareton Earnshaw', she asked me to be her messenger and bear the present to him.

'And tell him, if he'll take it, I'll come and teach him to read it,' she said, 'and if he refuses, I'll go upstairs and never trouble him again.'

I carried it, and repeated the message. Hareton would not open his fingers, so I laid it on his knee. I returned to my work.

Cathy leaned her head and arms on the table until she heard the slight noise of the covering being removed, then she crept away and seated herself quietly by her cousin. He trembled, and his face shone. All his rudeness had left him. He could not at first find the courage to say a word in reply to her questioning look.

'Say you forgive me, Hareton, do!'

He murmured something that could not be heard.

'And you'll be my friend?'

'But you'll be ashamed of me every day of your life,' he answered, 'and I can't bear it.'

'So you won't be my friend?' she said, smiling sweet as sugar.

I could hear no further talk but, on looking round again, I saw two happy shining faces bent over the pages of the accepted book.

The friendship grew rapidly, though there were sometimes interruptions. Hareton could not be educated with a wish, and my young lady was not a model of patience. But as both their minds had the same idea – one loving and desiring good opinion, the other loving and desiring to give praise – they managed in the end to make a success of their relationship.

Chapter 34   Two or Three Bushes

On the day following that Monday, Cathy arrived downstairs before me and went out into the garden, where she had seen her cousin doing some light work. When I called her in to breakfast, I saw that she had persuaded him to clear a large area of ground of some fruit bushes, and they were busy planning to bring some plants over from the Grange.

I was worried at the change that had been made in a short half-hour. The fruit bushes were Joseph's work and she had fixed her choice of a flowerbed in the middle of them.

'There! That will be shown to the master!' I exclaimed. 'We shall have a fine explosion, see if we don't!'

'I'd forgotten they were Joseph's,' answered Hareton, 'but I'll tell him I did it.'

We always ate our meals with Mr Heathcliff. I took the mistress's place in making tea and serving the meat. Cathy usually sat by me, but today she crept nearer to Hareton.

'Now mind you don't talk to and notice your cousin too much,' was my whispered advice as we entered the room. 'It will certainly annoy Mr Heathcliff, and he'll be angry with you both.'

'I'm not going to,' she answered.

A minute later, she had moved closer to him and was pushing flowers into the food on his plate.

He dared not speak, he dared hardly look, but she went on until he could not keep back a smile. I looked disapproving, and she looked in the direction of the master, whose mind was occupied with other matters, as his expression showed. She became serious, but soon afterwards she started her nonsense again. At last, Hareton laughed softly.

Mr Heathcliff turned and looked at our faces. Cathy met his eye with her usual look of fear mixed with scorn.

'It is just as well that you are out of my reach,' he exclaimed. 'What makes you stare at me with those eyes? Down with them! I thought I had cured you of laughing.'

'It was I,' murmured Hareton.

Mr Heathcliff looked at him for a bit, and then silently went on with his breakfast. We had nearly finished when Joseph appeared at the door, showing plainly by his trembling lip and furious eyes that the attack on his precious bushes had been discovered. His jaws worked like those of a cow, and his speech was difficult to understand. Heathcliff listened impatiently to his long string of complaints.

'Is the fool drunk?' he asked at last. 'Hareton, is it you he's finding fault with?'

'I've pulled up two or three bushes,' replied the young man.

'And why have you pulled them up?'

Cathy put in her word.

'We wanted to plant some flowers there,' she said. 'I'm the only person to blame.'

'And who gave you permission to touch a thing about the place?' demanded Heathcliff, greatly surprised. 'And who ordered you to obey her?' he added, turning to Hareton.

The young man was speechless. His cousin replied: 'You shouldn't mind me having a few yards of earth to make pretty, when you have taken all my land!'

'Your land! You never had any!'

'And my money,' she continued, returning his angry look and biting into the last piece of her breakfast.

'Silence!' he exclaimed. 'Finish, and go!'

'And Hareton's land, and his money,' she went on. 'Hareton and I are friends now, and I shall tell him all about you!'

The master seemed unable to reply for a moment. He became pale and stood up, eyeing her with an expression of murderous hate.

'If you strike me, Hareton will strike you,' she said, 'so you may as well sit down!'

Hareton tried in a whisper to persuade her to go.

'He'll not obey you any more, you wicked man,' said Cathy, 'and he'll soon hate you as much as I do!'

'Be quiet!' murmured the young man. 'I won't hear you speak like that to him.'

'But you'll not let him strike me?'

'Come away,' he whispered.

It was too late. Heathcliff had caught hold of her. He had his hand in her hair. Hareton attempted to free the curls, begging him not to hurt her this time. Heathcliff's black eyes flashed. He seemed ready to tear Cathy to pieces. I was just coming to help her, when all of a sudden his fingers loosened. He moved them to her arm and stared fixedly at her face. Then he pushed his hand over his eyes, stood a moment to control himself and, turning to Cathy, said with forced calmness: 'You must learn to avoid putting me into a fury, or I shall really murder you some time! Go to Mrs Dean, and stay with her. As to Hareton, if I see him listen to you, I'll send him to earn his living where he can get it. Your love will lose him the little he has! Leave me, all of you!'

I led my young lady out. She was too glad to escape to protest.

At dinnertime I advised her to have her meal upstairs, but as soon as he saw her empty seat Heathcliff sent me to call her.

He spoke to none of us, ate very little and went out directly afterwards, saying that he would not return before the evening.

Chapter 35   'A Poor Ending to My Struggles'

During Heathcliff's absence that day, the two new friends settled themselves in the house, and I heard Hareton speak firmly to his cousin, when she offered to tell the story of Heathcliff's behaviour towards his father. He said he would not allow a word to be spoken to him against Heathcliff. It did not matter what Heathcliff was like; he would stand by him, and he would rather she spoke badly of himself, as she used to do, than begin on Heathcliff. Cathy got annoyed at this, but he asked how she would like him to speak badly of *her* father, and then she understood that Hareton was joined to the master of Wuthering Heights by ties stronger than reason could break – chains, formed by habit, that it would be cruel to attempt to loosen. She showed a good heart, from that time, in avoiding both complaints and expressions of hate concerning Heathcliff, and admitted to me her sorrow that she had tried to raise bad feeling between him and Hareton. In fact, I don't believe she has ever breathed a word, in her cousin's hearing, against her enemy since.

When this slight disagreement was over, they were friends again and returned to being pupil and teacher. I came to sit with them, and I felt so comforted to watch them, that I did not notice how time was passing. You know, they both appeared to me, in some degree, as my children. I had been proud of one for a long time, and now, I was sure, the other would be an equal cause of satisfaction. His honest, warm and intelligent nature rapidly shook off the clouds of ignorance and degradation in which he had been brought up, and Cathy's sincere praise encouraged his steady progress. His brightening mind brightened his face too. I could hardly believe it was the same person I had seen on the day when I discovered my little lady at Wuthering Heights after her ride to the rocks.

While I admired, and they worked on, evening came and the master returned. He came on us unexpectedly, entering by the front way, and he had a full view of the three of us before we could raise our heads. I thought there was never a pleasanter or more harmless sight. The red firelight shone gently on the two young heads and showed their faces lit up with the eager interest of children, because though he was twenty-three and she eighteen, each had so much that was new to learn and to feel that neither appeared grown-up.

They lifted their heads together. Perhaps you haven't noticed that their eyes are exactly alike, and they are those of Catherine Earnshaw. The present Cathy has no other likeness to her, except a certain width of forehead. With Hareton, the likeness goes further, and at that moment it was particularly clear because his mind was unusually active. I suppose that this likeness affected Mr Heathcliff. He walked to the fireplace, noticeably upset. He looked at the young man and took the book from his hand, looking quickly at the page and returning it without any remark. He made a sign to Cathy to leave. Her companion soon followed, and I too was about to go but he ordered me to sit still.

'It's a poor ending, isn't it,' he remarked, after a minute of silence, 'an unsatisfactory ending to my struggles? I turn all my energies to planning the destruction of the two families, and when everything is ready I find that the will to act has disappeared! My old enemies have not beaten me, and now would be the exact moment to revenge myself on their children. I could do it and no one could prevent me! But what is the use? It's not that I am showing generosity – I have lost the power to enjoy their destruction, and I am too lazy to destroy for nothing.

'Nelly, a strange change is taking place. I'm in its shadow at present. I take so little interest in my daily life that I hardly remember to eat and drink. Those two who have left the room are the only objects that have a clear appearance to me and that appearance causes me pain. About *her* I won't speak, and I don't desire to think. Her presence maddens me. *He* affects me differently.

'Five minutes ago, Hareton seemed a living picture of my youth. I felt for him in a variety of ways. In the first place, his extreme likeness to Catherine connected him with her in my mind. Not that this is his most powerful effect on my imagination, because what is *not* connected with her, to me? I cannot look down at this floor without seeing her face shaped on the stones! In every cloud, in every tree, I see her! The most ordinary faces of men and women deceive me with a likeness. The whole world is a horrible collection of reminders that she did exist, and that I have lost her!

'Well, Hareton's appearance was the ghost of my undying love, of my degradation, my pride, my happiness and my suffering . . . but it is madness to repeat these thoughts to you!'

'What do you mean by a change, Mr Heathcliff?' I said, worried by his manner, though he was neither in danger of losing his senses nor of dying. According to my judgement, he was quite strong and healthy and, as to his imagination, he had always from childhood taken pleasure in strange ideas. He might have strange fixed ideas on the subject of his lost love, but on every other point his brain was as sharp as mine.

'I shall not know until it comes,' he said.

'You have no feeling of illness, have you?'

'No, Nelly, I have not.'

'Then you are not afraid of death?'

'Afraid? No!' he replied. 'I have neither fear nor hope of death. Why should I? With my strength and healthy way of life, I ought to remain on the earth until there is hardly a black hair on my head! But I can't continue in this condition! I have to remind myself to breathe – almost to remind my heart to beat! I have a single desire, and my whole being is eager to realize it! I'm certain that it will be realized – and soon – because it has eaten up my existence. Oh, God! It is a long fight. I wish it were over.'

He began to walk restlessly up and down, murmuring terrible things to himself, until I began to believe that a sense of guilt had filled his heart with pain. I asked myself how it would end.

Chapter 36   The Change Comes

For some days after that evening, Mr Heathcliff avoided meeting us at meals, but he would not agree to allow Hareton and Cathy to eat elsewhere. He disliked giving way so completely to his feelings, preferring instead to be absent himself, and taking food about once in twenty-four hours.

One night, after the family were in bed, I heard him go downstairs and out of the front door. In the morning he was still away. It was April then, the weather was sweet and warm, the grass green, and the two apple trees on the southern wall in full flower. Cathy suggested that I bring a chair and do my work outside, and she persuaded Hareton to dig and arrange her little garden, now moved to this corner to satisfy Joseph. I was enjoying the blue sky and the warm sun when my young lady, who had run down near the gate to get some flower roots for a border, returned and informed us that Mr Heathcliff was coming in.

'And he spoke to me,' she said, with surprise. 'He told me to get away as fast as I could. But he looked so different that I stopped for a moment to stare at him.'

'How?' asked Hareton.

'Why, almost bright and cheerful – no, more than that – very much excited, and wild, and glad!'

I made an excuse to go in. Heathcliff stood at the open door. He was pale, and he trembled, but he had a strange joyful light in his eyes.

'Will you have some breakfast?' I said. 'You must be hungry.'

'No, I'm not hungry,' he answered, rather scornfully.

'I don't think it right to wander out of doors at night. It isn't wise, at least, in this wet season. You'll catch a bad cold.'

'Nothing that I can't bear.'

I noticed that he was breathing very fast and hard.

At midday he sat down to dinner with us and received a plate of food from my hands. He took his knife and fork, and was going to begin, when he suddenly laid them on the table, looked eagerly towards the window, then rose and went out. We saw him walking in the garden, and soon Hareton said he would go and ask him why he would not eat. He thought we had upset him in some way.

'Well, is he coming?' cried Cathy, when her cousin returned.

'No, but he's not angry. He told me to return to you, and asked how I could want the company of anybody else.'

I set his plate to keep warm by the fire. After an hour or two he re-entered, the same unnatural appearance of joy under his dark forehead, the same bloodless colour, and his teeth showing now and then in a kind of smile, his body shivering, not as one shivers from cold and weakness, but as a tight-stretched string trembles at a touch.

'Have you heard any good news lately, Mr Heathcliff?' I exclaimed. 'You look strangely excited.'

'Where would good news come from to me? And Nelly, once and for all, let me beg you to warn Hareton and the other one to keep away from me. I wish to have this place to myself.'

'Tell me why you are so strange, Mr Heathcliff!'

'I'll tell you. Last night, I was in misery. Today I am within sight of my heaven. I have my eyes on it. Only three feet separate me from it! And now you'd better go.'

I took away his uneaten dinner, more uncertain than ever.

He did not leave the house again, and at eight o'clock I thought I had better carry a candle and supper to him.

He was leaning against the edge of an open window. The fire had burned to ashes, and the room was filled with the cold, wet air, so still that the murmur of the stream down at Gimmerton could be heard. I began shutting the windows, one after another, until I came to him.

'Must I close this?' I asked, in order to call his attention.

The light flashed on his face as I spoke. What a terrible shock I got! Those deep black eyes, that smile, that deathly paleness! It appeared to me to be not Mr Heathcliff but an evil spirit, and in my terror I let the candle go out, and it left me in darkness.

'Yes, close it,' he said, in his familiar voice. 'There, that was foolish of you. Be quick, and bring another candle.'

I hurried out in a state of fear, and told Joseph to take a light. He went, and came back at once with the supper in his hand, explaining that the master was going to bed, and would not eat until morning.

We heard him go upstairs immediately. He did not enter his usual room, but turned into the one with the big closed-in wooden bed, where Catherine Earnshaw used to sleep.

It was a troubled night for me. In my mind I went over and over the strange life and nature of Heathcliff, remembering how I had looked after him as a child and watched him grow up.

'But where did he come from, the little dark thing, sheltered by a good man to the ruin of his family?' I asked myself. And I began, half dreaming, to imagine some suitable parents for him.

◆

Next morning, I prepared breakfast as usual for the household, and as Cathy and Hareton preferred taking theirs out of doors, I laid a little table for their use.

On re-entering, I found Mr Heathcliff downstairs. He and Joseph were talking about some farming business. He gave clear, exact directions concerning the matter discussed, but he spoke rapidly and had the same excited expression as on the day before. When Joseph left the room, he took his usual seat and I put coffee in front of him. He pulled it nearer, and then rested his arms on the table and looked at the opposite wall, fixing his feverish eyes on one particular place with such eager interest that he stopped breathing for half a minute.

'Come, now,' I exclaimed, pushing some bread against his hand. 'Eat, and drink that, while it is still hot.'

He didn't notice me, but still he smiled.

'Mr Heathcliff! Master!' I cried. 'Don't, I beg you, stare as if you saw a ghost!'

'Don't, I beg you, shout so loud,' he replied. 'Turn round, and tell me, are we by ourselves?'

'Of course.'

With a quick movement of his hand he made a space in front among the breakfast things, and leaned forward to stare more comfortably.

Now, I saw, he was not looking at the wall. It seemed that he kept his eyes fixed on something about two yards away. And whatever it was, it communicated, seemingly, both pleasure and pain, in extremes; at least the expression on his face suggested that idea. The imagined object was not fixed either.

His eyes followed it with unfailing watchfulness and, even when he was speaking to me, were never turned away. I reminded him of his food, but without success.

I sat, a model of patience, trying to attract his attention, until he became annoyed and got up. He left the house, passed slowly down the garden path, and disappeared through the gate.

The hours crept by. Another evening came. I did not go to rest until late, and when I did I couldn't sleep.

Heathcliff returned after midnight and shut himself up in the sitting room. I listened and, after a time, dressed and came downstairs.

I could hear Heathcliff walking restlessly up and down in the room. The silence was frequently broken by strange cries and the sound of murmured speech. The only word I could catch was the name of Catherine, joined with some wild word of love or suffering, and spoken as one would speak to a person who was present — low and serious and torn from the depths of his soul.

I hadn't the courage to walk in, so I made a noise while attending to the kitchen fire. He opened the door then and said: 'Nelly, come here. Is it morning?'

'It is striking four,' I answered.

'Come and light me a fire.'

He wandered up and down, breathing rapidly.

'When day breaks, I'll send for Green,' he said. 'I wish to make inquiries of him concerning some matters of law, while I can still act calmly. I have not made my will yet, and I cannot decide how to leave my property. I wish I could destroy it from the face of the earth!'

'I wouldn't talk so, Mr Heathcliff,' I said. 'Leave your will for a time. You'll still live to be sorry for your many unjust acts! You're in a nervous state, and the way you've passed these three days would take anyone's strength away. Do take some food, and some rest.'

'You might as well urge a man struggling in the water to rest within arm's length of the shore! I must reach it first, and then I'll rest. Well, never mind Mr Green. As to my unjust acts, I've done none and I'm sorry for nothing. I'm too happy, but I'm not happy enough. My soul's happiness kills my body, but does not satisfy itself.'

'Happy, master?' I cried. 'If you would hear me without being angry, I might offer you some advice.'

'Give it.'

'You should know, Mr Heathcliff, that from the time you were about thirteen years old, you have led a wicked, irreligious life. Could it be harmful now to send for a priest to guide you, and help you to a change of heart?'

'I'm more grateful than angry, Nelly, as you have reminded me of the manner in which I desire to be buried. It is to be carried to the churchyard in the evening, and to be laid by her side. You and Hareton may follow my body, and make sure, particularly, that the gravedigger obeys my directions concerning the two coffins! No priest need come, nor need any prayer be said over my grave. I tell you, I have nearly reached my heaven.'

Hearing the other members of the household getting up, he rose and went to his own room.

Chapter 37   The End of Heathcliff

That same afternoon, while Joseph and Hareton were at their work, he came into the kitchen and, with a wild look, told me to come and sit with him, as he wanted somebody there. I refused, telling him plainly that his strange talk frightened me.

'I believe you think I'm an evil spirit,' he said, 'something too horrible to live under a respectable roof!' Then, turning to Cathy, who hid behind me, he added, half jokingly, 'Will *you* come, girl? I'll not hurt you. No! To you, I've made myself hateful. Well, there is *one* who will not move away from my company! Oh, God! She's without pity! It's too much for flesh and blood to bear, even mine.'

He asked no one else to stay with him. At sunset he went to his room, and all through the night we heard him murmuring to himself. Hareton was anxious to enter, but I told him to fetch the doctor.

When he came, Heathcliff would not open the door. He said he was better and wanted to be left alone, so Doctor Kenneth went away.

The following evening was very wet. It poured until daybreak and, as I took my morning walk round the house, I noticed the master's window was open and the rain blowing straight in. He must be up, I thought. He could not be in bed, as the rain would be all over it. I decided to go and look.

Having succeeded in gaining entrance with another key, I ran to open the doors of the old bed, as the room was empty. Quickly pushing them to one side, I looked in. Mr Heathcliff was there – lying on his back. His eyes met mine, so steady and fierce, that I made a movement of fear, and then he seemed to smile.

I could not think that he was dead, but his face and throat were washed with rain, the bedclothes were wet through, and he was perfectly still. I put my fingers on one of his hands. Then my doubts left me.

I cried out for Joseph, who came and fell on his knees and gave thanks that the lawful master and the ancient family were once more in possession of their rights.

I felt unhappy and upset by the terrible event, and my memory returned to former times with a sort of unbearable sadness. But poor Hareton, the most wronged, was the only one who really suffered much. He sat by the body all night and kissed the fierce, scornful face that everybody avoided looking at, and suffered the strong grief that comes naturally from a generous heart.

PART 6   GOODBYE TO WUTHERING HEIGHTS

Mr Lockwood's last words

Chapter 38   The Dead Are at Peace

Mrs Dean was silent for a minute at the end of her story.

'They are going to the Grange, then?' I asked.

'Yes, as soon as they are married, and that will be on New Year's Day.'

'And who will live here?'

'Well, Joseph will take care of the house, with perhaps a boy to keep him company. They will live in the kitchen, and the rest of the house will be shut up.'

'For the use of any ghosts that choose to return to it,' I remarked.

'No, Mr Lockwood,' said Nelly, shaking her head, 'I believe that the dead are at peace.'

At that moment the garden gate opened. The wanderers were returning.

'They are afraid of nothing,' I said.

As they stepped up to the door and paused to take a last look at the moon, or rather at each other, by her light, I felt a desire to avoid them and, quickly saying goodbye to Mrs Dean, I passed through the kitchen and left.

My walk home was lengthened by a turn in the direction of the churchyard. I looked for, and soon discovered, the three stones at the head of the graves on the slope next to the moor: the middle one grey, and half buried in wild plants; Edgar Linton's only covered at the foot with grass, and Heathcliff's still brown earth.

I remained near them. I watched the insects among the wild flowers. I listened to the soft wind breathing through the grass. And I asked myself how anyone could ever imagine unquiet rest for the sleepers below that quiet ground.

ACTIVITIES

Chapters 1–4

Before you read

1 Check the meanings of these words in your dictionary.

candle   household   moor   tenant   fierce
landlord   murmur   wicked   gypsy   mistress   shiver

  a Which words refer to people?

  b What is the relationship between a landlord and a tenant?

Are these sentences true or false? Correct the false ones.

  c A *moor* is an area of land which is covered with forests.

  d A *mouse* is a very fierce animal.

  e You use a *candle* to give light.

  f You *shiver* when you are hungry.

  g If you *murmur* something, you say it very loudly.

  h A person who is *wicked* behaves in a way that is morally wrong.

After you read

2 Who are these people?

  a Mr Lockwood

  b Mr Heathcliff

  c Joseph and Zillah

  d Mrs Dean

  e Catherine Earnshaw

  f Hareton Earnshaw

3 Discuss what you know about Heathcliff's appearance and character and his past and present lifestyles.

4 Take the parts of Mrs Dean and Mr Lockwood.

  Student A: You are Mrs Dean. Ask Mr Lockwood questions about the night he spent at Wuthering Heights.

  Student B: You are Mr Lockwood. Answer Mrs Dean's questions and discuss your experiences with her.

Chapters 5–10

Before you read

5 The title of the next part of the book is 'The First Catherine'.
What do you think Mrs Dean's story will be about?

6 Find these words in your dictionary. They are all in the story.

*creep   degrade   exclaim   fury   misery   naughty
scorn   superior   weep*

Match the words with the correct meanings.

a great unhappiness
b disobedient
c treat someone without respect
d move quietly and carefully
e cry
f say something suddenly and loudly
g better than another person or thing
h extreme anger
i feeling that someone is stupid or not as good as someone
else

After you read

7 Who is speaking to whom, and what are they talking about?

a 'You must take this as a gift of God, though it's as dark as if
it came from the devil.'
b 'I'd not exchange my condition here for Edgar Linton's at
Thrushcross Grange, not for a thousand lives!'
c 'Away, you gypsy! What! Are you trying to make yourself
look like your superiors!'
d 'I don't care how long I wait, if only I can do it in the end.'
e 'It's no company at all, when people know nothing, and say
nothing.'
f 'Can I stay after you have struck me?'
g 'In my soul and in my heart, I'm certain I'm wrong.'

8 Discuss the relationship between Catherine and Heathcliff.
How realistic do you find it? How can it be explained?

9 Take the parts of Catherine and Heathcliff and act out the conversation that you think they will have at their next meeting.

10 Compare life at Wuthering Heights with life at Thrushcross Grange.

Chapters 11–20

Before you read

11 Look in the Contents list at the titles of Chapters 11–20. What do you think the main events of this part of the book will be?

12 Find these words in your dictionary:

coffin   ignorant

a What shape is a *coffin*?

b If you are *ignorant* about something, you have no .... about it.

After you read

13 Answer the questions.

a How long does Heathcliff stay away for?

b Where does he live on his return?

c What are the effects of his influence on young Hareton?

d What causes Catherine to quarrel with Heathcliff?

e Where does Isabella go when she leaves Thrushcross Grange?

f Why does Hindley Earnshaw allow Heathcliff to stay with him?

g How does Catherine die?

h Who are her last conscious words addressed to?

i What is her last, unconscious speech about?

j Whose hair does she take to the grave?

k Why does Isabella leave Wuthering Heights?

l How does Heathcliff treat Hindley?

14 How does Heathcliff manage to claim:

a Hindley's property, including Wuthering Heights?

b Hareton Earnshaw?

15 Explain Heathcliff's remark to Catherine:

'I love my murderer – but yours! How can I?'

Chapters 21–28

Before you read

  16 Who are Cathy Linton's parents? Who are the parents of her
       two cousins? What do we know about these last two children?

After you read

  17 Complete these sentences with the right names.

   a When .... dies, Edgar Linton goes to fetch ....
   b .... lives at Thrushcross Grange in the care of her father
    and ....
   c Wuthering Heights is the home of .... and ....;
    .... is also forced to live there.
   d .... and .... write secret notes to each other.
   e It is ....'s plan that .... and .... should marry.
   f During ....'s illness, ... makes frequent visits
    alone to Wuthering Heights.
   g .... finally agrees that the cousins should meet under the
    protection of ....
   h .... and .... are both very ill.
   i When .... dies, Thrushcross Grange will belong to
    .... When he dies, it will belong to ....

  18 Compare the characters and appearances of Hareton and Linton.

Chapters 29–38

Before you read

  19 At this stage in the story, which of the characters do you feel
       sorry for and why? Which, if any, of the characters do you like?

After you read

  20 Explain why:
   a Heathcliff wants Edgar to die before Linton.
   b Heathcliff hits Cathy and pushes Nelly over.
   c Edgar Linton is unable to make a new will.

d Heathcliff damages Catherine's coffin.
  e Cathy does not leave Wuthering Heights after Linton's death.
  f Cathy finally decides to be friends with Hareton.
  g Hareton cannot hate Heathcliff.
  h Heathcliff goes mad.

21 Imagine you are Nelly. After Heathcliff's death, explain to Hareton how and why Heathcliff cheated him.

Writing

22 Is it true that Heathcliff is an evil man for whom the reader can have no sympathy?

23 Compare the two Catherines. How are their characters similar? How are they different?

24 How does Heathcliff use violence and fear to achieve his aims?

25 How effective is Heathcliff's influence on Hareton?

26 Write a letter from Edgar Linton, as he is dying, to his daughter Cathy, expressing his hopes and fears for her future.

27 How important to the story is the setting of the lonely houses and the wild moors?

Answers for the Activities in this book are available from your local office or alternatively write to: Penguin Readers Marketing Department, Pearson Education, Edinburgh Gate, Harlow, Essex CM20 2JE.